JOURNEY TO THE

SEA

EDITED BY

SARAH BROWN

GIL MCNEIL AND HUGO TAGHOLM

EBURY PRESS

First published in Great Britain in 2005

10 9 8 7 6 5 4 3 2 1

First published by
Ebury Press
Random House, 20 Vauxhall Bridge Road, London SW1V 2SA

Random House Australia (Pty) Limited
20 Alfred Street, Milsons Point, Sydney, New South Wales 2061, Australia

Random House New Zealand Limited
18 Poland Road, Glenfield, Auckland 10, New Zealand

Random House South Africa (Pty) Limited
Endulini, 5A Jubilee Road, Parktown 2193, South Africa

The Random House Group Limited Reg. No. 954009

www.randomhouse.co.uk

A CIP catalogue record for this book is available from the British Library.

Cover Design by the Two Associates
Text design and typesetting by Textype

ISBN 0091900697

Papers used by Ebury Press are natural, recyclable products made from wood grown in sustainable forests.

Printed and bound in Great Britain by Cox and Wyman Ltd, Reading, Berks.

£1 for each copy sold donated to PiggyBankKids (charity registration number 1092312)

'Sea-Fever' by John Masefield reproduced by kind permission of the Society of Authors, Literary Representatives of the Estate of John Masefield.

'The Beach Butler' by Ruth Rendell © Kingsmarkham Enterprises Ltd.

This anthology has been compiled and edited by Sarah Brown, Gil McNeil and Hugo Tagholm. PiggyBankKids will be supporting Special Olympics Great Britain with the publication of this book, and will receive £1 for every copy sold.

For further information please contact:
PiggyBankKids
16 Lincoln's Inn Fields
London WC2A 3ED
www.piggybankkids.org

ACKNOWLEDGEMENTS

Our grateful thanks to the authors who have contributed to this collection, and to their agents; to everyone at Ebury Press, especially Gail Rebuck, Hannah MacDonald, Sarah Bennie, Rae Shirvington, Fiona MacIntyre and Claire Kingston; Chris Hooper and Karen Bunton at Special Olympics Great Britain; and the PiggyBankKids Board of Trustees, Swraj Paul, Mary Goudie, David Boutcher and Helen Scott Lidgett.

Personal thanks are due to Gordon Brown; Joe McNeil; John and Sally Tagholm; Sarah Coombs; Margaret Foster; and Anne-Marie Piper.

CONTENTS

INTRODUCTION

SARAH BROWN

Most of us have childhood memories of time spent by the sea, from holidays to day trips, in sunshine or stormy weather, and damp sandwiches and sandy blankets usually play their part in these memories. At various times in my childhood my brothers and I holidayed at North Berwick, Hunstanton and Walberswick, Brighton and Llandudno, burying each other in the sand or skimming stones across the water; and now when I take a break from 11 Downing Street to go to Scotland with my family, one of the things I look forward to most is the view over the Firth of Forth. The sight of water when you wake up in the morning is definitely good for the soul. The sea also has a wider role in our collective heritage than simple reminiscence and relaxation; from Coleridge's Ancient Mariner, alone on his 'wide wide sea', to Defoe's Robinson Crusoe, from the history of heroic figures like Admiral Nelson and Grace

Darling to the stories of Dunkirk and the folklore of fishermen and lifeboat crews, our history is full of the brave adventures of our island race. Stories of people who push themselves to the limit, facing great peril and encountering great beauty. People who conquer overwhelming odds but never give up, like the people I met when I attended the Special Olympics World Summer Games in Dublin last year. The Games were the culmination of the year-round training and competition undertaken by people with a learning disability, and I was struck by just how inspiring the opening ceremony was, seeing seven thousand athletes from over a hundred and fifty countries proudly marching behind their country's flag. Not only for those taking part, but also for their families and carers, who got to see so many people who at first glance might not appear destined for glory being brave enough to give it a go, and bringing a real sense of achievement both to themselves and to everyone associated with their efforts. It was a real privilege to be there, and after meeting the team at Special Olympics Great Britain everyone at PiggyBankKids was determined to help them in their efforts to increase the number of athletes, coaches and volunteers and to improve the quality and range of sports on offer.

Since I launched PiggyBankKids in 2002 we have raised over a million pounds for our ongoing projects, including the Jennifer Brown Research Fund which supports a perinatal research laboratory based at the Royal Infirmary in Edinburgh. We have worked on partnership projects with other charities to support mentoring and volunteering, family services, and advice for one-parent families. Last year we launched our new fundraising initiative, The Big Night In, which will help us fund all our core projects and enable us to expand the range of charities we help. Our aims at PiggyBankKids are simple: to support and strengthen charities working to improve opportunities for children and young people across the UK. So we are especially proud to be working with Special Olympics Great Britain, which has such a positive approach to providing ever greater facilities for their young people and creating an environment that encourages previously unimaginable achievements.

Thank you so much for buying this book and helping us to raise funds to promote the important work of Special Olympics Great Britain. I would like to thank my co-editors, Hugo Tagholm, our Programme Director at PiggyBankKids, who's a keen surfer, and Gil McNeil, our Publishing Director, who is still trying to get the sand out of the back of her car after her son discovered the joys of surfing last summer. Most of all I would like to thank our brilliant writers, who all so generously agreed to donate their work for free. I am sure you will enjoy reading their fantastic stories as much as I have.

Sarah Brown
PiggyBankKids
February 2005

'LET ME WIN, BUT IF I
CANNOT WIN, LET ME BE
BRAVE IN THE ATTEMPT'

CHRIS HOOPER
Executive Director,
Special Olympics Great Britain

To COMPETE WELL IN ANY sport, or indeed in life itself, requires inspiration, determination, confidence and self-belief. For the average person the road often seems tough, but the attainment of success is even more of a challenge when you have a learning disability. For those with a learning disability the true ideals of sportsmanship still exist and it remains an honour to compete, irrespective of the final result. The skills of winning and losing are taught to us all at a young age, but it is rare to find the qualities needed to accept defeat in the able-bodied population.

To witness seven thousand athletes from all over the world competing at the Special Olympics World Summer Games in Dublin in the summer of 2003 was incredible. This was the biggest sports event in the world in 2003, and with teams from Afghanistan to Australia it was truly global. The games were officially opened by Nelson Mandela in Croke Park stadium in Dublin, which was filled to capacity. Twenty-six different sports were contested. It was the pinnacle of years of preparation, and the realisation of a lifetime's dream for the athletes and their families.

This was so much more than a sports event – this was an opportunity for people with learning disabilities to make new friends, to gain confidence and to experience new cultures. Many of the athletes had never been away from their home villages and towns, let alone travelled to the other side of the globe. The Irish people embraced the games, and as a result many more learning-disabled people have been given the opportunity to get involved, as well as significant numbers of new volunteers eager to assist.

For many, of course, the World Games will always be a dream – the 400-metre race at the local park will be the height of their athletic achievement, but for them this will be just as special and just as defining.

The key to the success of Special Olympics is the extent of its reach beyond the sports field and the opportunities it can open up for people who have previously led sheltered lives and who have no belief in their own abilities. Many athletes are trained in leadership and are given the platform to become self-advocates and spokesmen and women for the organisation. Sport is a vehicle to achieve so much more in life – and it is not only the athletes who benefit. I have seen parents, siblings and teachers touched through their involvement and the success of others.

As Georgina Hulme, Special Olympics ambassador and athlete, says, 'As well as swimming, for the last twelve months I have also started coaching the young beginners at the end of every session, and it is very exciting to see their progress. Some of them, if not all, will be good enough to take part in galas this year. It is fair to say that my training through sport and the Special Olympics has allowed me to become more able to deal with other important matters in my life, particularly college work. Special Olympics has helped me to achieve many of my dreams and ambitions.'

In Great Britain, Special Olympics is still relatively small, with only five thousand athletes taking part in regular training and sports competition. Potentially, however, there are over a million learning-disabled people in Great Britain, and over the next couple of years it is our goal to recruit another five thousand into the programme. The focus of the growth will be among the school-age population in order to get young parents and volunteers involved whose energy can drive Special Olympics forward.

Sailing and kayaking are both very popular sports within Special Olympics, and I know that the anecdotes and memories recalled in this book, from some of our greatest mariners, will provide great inspiration to our athletes. We are a nation surrounded by the sea, a treasure that has protected us and provided pleasure over many generations.

The next National Summer Games for Special Olympics GB will take place in Glasgow, 1–9 July 2005. The games are expected to attract three thousand athletes with learning disabilities, together with a thousand coaches and at least three thousand parents, carers, supporters and friends, from nineteen regions throughout Great Britain. Over the eight days, the athletes will compete in twenty-three sports at eleven venues in and around the city of Glasgow.

The opportunity to be the beneficiary charity from the sales of this wonderful book is fantastic, and I would like to sincerely thank Sarah Brown and PiggyBankKids for supporting Special Olympics.

MOMENTO

ANDREW MOTION

I have forgotten the beach
Where I knelt in the blinding wind,
And this perfectly round white stone
Rose glittering into my reach.

Here it is now on our shelf
Like an egg, or an eye, or a clue
Dropped from the lips of the sea
To something besides itself.

Yes I have forgotten the day,
The sun, the wind, the waves,
And even your loving look –
But I still took something away.

SMILES

ALEXANDER MCCALL SMITH

SHE ARRIVED IN BANGKOK NOT knowing what to expect. Her husband knew the place, as he had made a number of business trips there over the years.

'You'll be happy there,' he said. 'I promise you. People are. And the Thais are very friendly. You'll see.'

'But the traffic,' she said. 'And all that noise. The children . . . '

He touched her arm in reassurance. 'There's traffic in Sydney too, remember. And the children will be fine. The firm will provide us with a maid – two, if you want. You'll have all the help you need with the children.'

He had been right. She liked living in Bangkok, and soon stopped missing Sydney, where they came from. It was easy to keep in touch with Australian friends, too, as they were often able to break their overseas journeys with a stop in Bangkok.

'They stay the perfect length of time for guests,' she wrote in a letter. 'Three days to catch up on things and then they move on. Guests are like fish, aren't they? After three days they begin to go off.'

Her husband enjoyed his job. He was now in the

highest echelons of an international firm of accountants, and he had been put in charge of the Bangkok office. They mixed in elevated financial circles, with parties and receptions at the houses of Thai plutocrats. They were popular in the society of the capital, and being photogenic her picture often appeared in the pages of the *Bangkok Tatler*. She went to charity auctions and fashion launches at the silk houses. And he liked this. 'It's good for business for you to be seen,' he said. 'Consider it work. Enjoy yourself.'

By the end of their fourth year there, when the boy was fifteen and the girl thirteen, they had become so established that the prospect of returning to Australia seemed something remote. Yes, they would go back, but not in the immediate future. The children had learned Thai and had their friends in Bangkok. They were doing well at their international school. They had better manners than their Australian contemporaries, and they had picked up that subtle physical grace which the Thais have. Australian teenagers seemed so ill at ease in the space they occupied, and were so gauche.

Then, on a Friday afternoon in the monsoon season, just as a heavy purple cloud was building up over the northern fringes of Bangkok and the air was heavy and humid, a woman from the office knocked at the door. She let her in and could tell immediately that something had happened. The Thais smiled in a particular way when they were distressed, and this was such a smile. It was always misread by foreigners – *farangs* as they called them – but she understood it very well and did not misinterpret it now.

Something very serious had happened. He's had an accident, she thought immediately. It's happened.

Every eight hours, somebody is killed in a traffic accident in Bangkok, so dense is the volume of cars, trucks, motorcycles. He had been in the car with his driver, apparently, and they had turned a corner into a narrow street. A small elephant and its keeper, a man from a hill tribe in the north, had been crossing the smaller road and the car had hit the elephant. The driver had been relatively unharmed, but her husband had been badly cut about the neck by flying glass. He had been dragged out, bleeding, and because there was no ambulance service to speak of had been put into a motorbike taxi, a *túk túk*, and driven to a nearby clinic, his driver trying to staunch the bleeding from his neck. He died in the brightly painted *túk túk* as it bumped its way along the pot-holed road.

There was an outcry from the firm and from those who had been campaigning to rid the city of elephants. 'They have no business in the city,' said a prominent member of the city administration. 'This is another example of what happens when you allow elephants to roam around in the city. These people who bring them in must be punished severely.' She did not want anybody to be punished. She saw a photograph in the *Bangkok Post* of the elephant that had caused the accident, and of his keeper, who looked so small beside his charge, and so intimidated by the presence of the two policemen in the background. The elephant's left foreleg, facing the camera, had a large gash in it, a laceration caused by the impact with the car. She stared at the photograph, and then turned the page quickly. But she turned back to the photograph and looked at it again, noticing the details, the shirt worn by the keeper, and the Buddhist amulet around his neck. He might have thought that this amulet had saved him, and made a victim of her husband instead, an anonymous *farang* whose car was going too fast anyway.

She could not go home. Her parents, who were retired and living in Melbourne, came over to stay with her, and helped. They urged her to return to Australia.

'You have to do it for the sake of the children,' they said. 'Think of them. What are they going to do here?'

'But it's for their sake that I'm staying,' she said. 'Look at them. They have all their friends. They're happy here. I don't want to uproot them.'

She stayed in Bangkok for a year, a year of pain and loneliness, which she tried to disguise for the children's sake. Her weepy moments, alone in the apartment overlooking the Chao Phraya river, were never witnessed by the children, although the boy sensed the depths of her distress, she felt, and put his arm about her at odd moments and hugged her to him. 'You have me,' he whispered. 'You're not alone. Remember that.'

A year after it happened she was invited by friends for a long weekend in their house on Samui, an island in the southern provinces. These friends, Americans who worked for one of the banks, were childless and her children, sensing a weekend without teenage company on Samui, opted to stay with friends in Bangkok.

The American couple lived on the west coast of the island, near a small village called Baan Thaling Ngam. They had spent a great deal on the house, which perched on the top of a hillside and was surrounded by palm trees. It had been built in the Thai style, but to the specifications of a Bangkok architect. The top storey had a large living room with a balcony overlooking an emerald-green sea; down below there were several bedrooms, with polished hardwood floors and windows with shutters against the heat. When the doors of the living room were opened, a warm breeze entered the house and kept it cool. This breeze carried the scent of the frangipani trees that had been planted in front of the house, a scent that made her think of expensive unguents and soaps.

'It's lovely here,' she said. 'So peaceful.'

'Yes,' they said. 'We're going to miss this place. We've put so much into it.'

'Miss it?'

'Paul's going back to New York. We've decided to sell.'

She said nothing, but that night, on the verandah, when they watched the sun burn down over the mainland, she decided that she would buy this house and live there. She would come down with the children during their school holidays and stay in the apartment in Bangkok during term.

'I'll buy this house from you,' she said suddenly.

And they had laughed. 'We hoped that you'd say that. We wanted somebody we knew to look after this place and its spirit house. Thank you.'

Many Thai houses had a small wooden spirit house in

the garden: a tiny building on a pole, resembling a bird-house, but decorated with ribbons and flowers and with offerings for the spirits. A well-kept spirit house would have happy spirits, who would be willing to stay. One that did not have regular offerings of fruit would be deserted by the spirits, spurned.

She returned to Bangkok with pictures of the house to show to the children. They approved of the idea. The boy, in particular, liked the sea. They had taken him on a num-ber of occasions to Hua Hin and Phuket, and it had been difficult to get him out of the water.

'Aquatic,' said her husband. 'Look at him. He's like some beautiful sea creature. An otter maybe.'

II

She was proved right about the children. They took to the house immediately and while they were on the island they largely forgot about their Bangkok friends. The boy took to fishing, and he struck up a friendship with a young man from a fishing community on one of the tiny islands off the shore of Samui. They could see this island from the house: it was a tiny lump of rock that rose sheer out of the sea and was topped by dense green jungle vegetation. At the base of this rock, the fishermen had built a few houses on stilts: houses made of palm straw and thick bamboo poles. On the edge of the cliff they had tied fishing poles with lines dangling down into the water, to catch lobsters and crabs, which they would take into the fish market on the large island. The boy sometimes went out with the young man, who was about his age, and fished from the side of the young man's father's longtail boat. She watched them set off from the beach, her son almost as browned by the sun as the other boy, and she thought of how her husband would have liked this. He found it more difficult to get over his natural reserve, and he spoke hesitantly to the locals. 'I feel so out of place with these people,' he said 'So . . . so large. It's as if I just don't get it.' She knew, though, that her son got it, whatever *it* was.

There were other foreigners in the area, and there was some social life amongst them. She got to know a couple, German artists, who had a villa further along the coast, and who entertained on a large scale. They held several parties each New Year, and it was at one of these that she met one of their friends, another Australian. He had been working in Bangkok and was between jobs. He was renting a house on Koh Samui for a couple of months before returning to Australia. She spoke to him for several hours at the party and invited him to the house the next day. He came, and met the children. She saw her son look at him, with attention, and then look away again.

This new friend returned her invitation.

'My house is not nearly as nice as this,' he said. 'But there's a pool, if the children want to come.'

The boy did not want to go. 'I'm going fishing,' he said. 'Samsook said he would collect me at the beach. We want to get some red snapper.'

She left them behind and went to his house. He showed

her the pool and the living room. He had a spirit house, too, but he had left it untended. A few flowers, now dried, placed there by a previous tenant, were lying at the spirits' doorway.

'The spirits will have moved out in disgust,' she said, half chiding him.

'I'll try to get them back,' he said, laughing. 'I'll make it up to them.'

She found herself comfortable in his company. He had an easy charm, and was a good conversationalist. She realised that since her husband's death there had been so much she had not been able to say, because there was nobody to say it to. She had forgotten, she realised, what it was like to sit down with a man, at the table, and talk to him about anything, small things that had happened during the day, things that people had said. And he sat there listening, and smiling; not the Thai smile with its numerous meanings, but a flickering smile that signalled intimacy and understanding.

He was divorced, and had been for some years. He had not wanted the divorce, and had tried to persuade his wife to stay. 'It was like a death,' he said, and then stopped, realising that this was tactless.

'It's all right,' she said. 'I'm sure it's just like that. I'm sure of it.'

They saw more and more of one another. He came to the house early in the mornings and stayed until late at night. They went out for dinner together at the nearby restaurant. The girl came with them sometimes, but the boy declined each invitation.

'I'm not sure if he approves of me,' he said to her.

She looked down. 'He's jealous. That's how it can be sometimes. I'm sorry. He'll get over it.'

He nodded. 'I've tried,' he said. 'I've tried to get through to him, but he doesn't seem to want it.'

'I'll have a word with him,' she said. 'It's difficult being a teenage boy, you know. They're all a bit like that.'

She went into her son's room that night. He was lying in bed, covered with a sheet, reading a book. He looked at her and smiled.

'I want to talk to you about Joe,' she said.

The boy's smile faded. He looked pointedly at the open pages of the book. 'What about Joe? What about him?'

'You should try to get to know him,' she said. 'You really should.'

The boy said nothing for a moment. 'He's going back to Australia, isn't he?'

'Yes, that's the general idea.'

'And he's going to ask you to go with him, isn't he?'

She caught her breath. They had talked about that, but she had no idea that her son would have worked that out. It was so recent, just the previous day, when he had asked her whether she would consider coming to live with him, and she had replied that she would. And then he had said: *What about leaving this country? Will that be all right?* And she had said, *Yes, there would be no difficulty in that.* She did not know Melbourne, but they could all be happy there, just as they had been happy in Sydney.

She reached out and put a hand on his shoulder, over the sheet. 'Sooner or later you're going to have to go back. This isn't really your country, you know. Australia's our country. If we go back with Joe, I'm sure you'd be happy. I'd be happy, you know. You do want me to be happy, too, don't you?'

'You could be happy here with me,' he said. 'Here in Thailand. What's wrong with that?'

She bent down and placed a kiss on his brow. 'Darling, sleep on it. Think about it. But give Joe a chance. Please. Just get to know him a little. Take him fishing. You and Samsook, take him fishing in that longtail boat.'

The boy said nothing, and so she stepped back and left the room.

III

The boy asked Joe to go fishing several days later. She saw them off at the beach. Joe stepped into the longtail boat, which was painted bright blue, with red lines round the rim and a garland of yellow flowers draped around the prow, for luck, for fish; for safety. Samsook was wearing a red sarong and smiled in welcome at Joe, bowing his head and performing the ritual Thai greeting with hands held together, as if in prayer. The boy said nothing, or very little, but looked at her in a strange way when the boat pushed off from the beach and into the light green water. She thought that she might call out to her son, to ask him what he wanted to say; but she did not wish to embarrass him.

He looked at her again as Samsook lowered the long drive-shaft into the water and engaged the engine; a look that was half regret, half reproach.

They were gone the whole day. At three in the afternoon she felt uneasy, and went outside, into the heat. She paused at the spirit house, which was positioned in a small clearing, surrounded by a clump of banana trees. There were fresh flowers on the small platform and a bowl of ripening plantains, as an offering. She had not put these there, so she concluded that it was her son. He was atten-tive to the spirit house, like a conscientious Thai.

At five in the afternoon, with a storm brewing off towards the mainland, she went down to the beach. There was a stiff breeze from the sea, and the fronds of the palms moved in sympathy with the wind. She looked out over the water, which was still calm but which was beginning to ruf-fle slightly with the effect of the wind. She saw the longtail boat in the distance, a low black shape like a tree trunk in the water, and she breathed a sigh of relief.

The boat nosed into the sand and Samsook jumped out, his bare feet in the sand and powdered shells. Joe followed him. He seemed to have lost his hat, and had tied a red ban-danna around his head to protect him from the sun. Her son was at the back of the boat, attending to the engine. He looked up and glanced at her, then looked back at the engine.

'You look like a pirate with that thing on your head,' she said to Joe, pointing at the bandanna.

He caught her eye. He was not smiling. 'Could you come with me back to my place,' he said. 'I want to talk.'

There was something in his tone that alarmed her, and she followed him back along the path to where he had parked his rented truck. They climbed in, and he drove quickly down the track that led to the main road. She noticed that his lips were pursed and that there was a scratch along the side of his cheek.

'Has something happened?' she asked.

'I don't want to talk just yet,' he said. 'We'll talk when we get to my place.'

'You've cut your cheek,' she said. 'I'll put something on it for you. You have to watch cuts in this heat.'

It was no more than a ten-minute drive to his house, but he drove fast and it seemed that they were there in no time. When they arrived, he nodded for her to follow him.

'You're being a bit mysterious,' she said as they mounted the steps into the building. 'At least you could tell me what . . .'

He turned to her and spoke. She saw that he was shaking. 'He tried to kill me,' he said. 'He pushed me in and they went off.'

She stood quite still. It was difficult for her to take this in. 'Who tried?' she said. 'Tried to do what?'

'Your son,' he said, pointing a finger at her. 'He gave me a shove when I was standing up to free a line. I hit the side of my head as I went in – hence this.' He touched the wound gently. 'And then they went off. I saw them. But they had an argument – I saw it, hands waving, everything, and Samsook grabbed the controls and they came back and he hauled me back in. Your son was all apologies. It was an accident, he said. I should not have stood up in the boat like that. He was turning the boat to get into a position to rescue me. That's what he said.'

She stood and looked at him. She wanted to say, *This is not true; it simply isn't true*, but the words would not come.

'We were way out,' he went on. 'Really far. If it hadn't been for Samsook, then I don't know. With the storm coming on, nobody would have seen me. The fishing boats were all running for shelter.'

She closed her eyes. It could not be true. Her son would not try to murder Joe. He was sixteen. He was a boy.

He reached out and touched her gently on the arm. 'This won't work, you know. I couldn't ask you to choose between your son and me. I couldn't ask you that. I'm very sorry.'

'I'll talk to him,' she said. 'I'm sure that there's been a misunderstanding.'

'No,' he said. 'I'm very sorry. I'm going to pack up and go back to Bangkok. I can't be involved in . . . I can't be involved in this. Not with him. Sorry.'

He moved away from her, up the steps and into the house, but he stopped short of the door.

'I'm sorry,' he said. 'I'm not thinking straight. I'll run you back to your house. Give me a moment.'

She returned to the beach. Her son was still there, with Samsook. They had dragged the longtail boat up onto the sand, for safety, and were doing something to the engine. She saw that Samsook had a can of oil in his hand. He looked up at her when he saw her coming and said something to her son.

She walked over to the two boys. 'Samsook,' she said. 'What happened? What happened?' She struggled for the Thai words as she pointed out towards the sea.

Samsook looked at her in surprise. Then he looked at the other boy, and there was a sign. She was sure of it; there was a sign. 'He fell into the water,' he said. 'Like that. Splash. We picked him up and came back. He does not know the sea.'

She moved towards him. 'Is that true? He says that he was pushed into the sea and that you boys wanted to leave him.'

Samsook looked at her, and smiled. He moved slightly away. This was the smile that meant, *You're embarrassing me.* He smiled again. It was the same message.

She turned to her son. He had been busying himself with the engine, as if indifferent to what she had said to Samsook.

'Is that true?' she said to him, her voice raised. 'Did you push him in? Did you?'

The boy stood up. She noticed now, and every time she looked at him, how he seemed to have become a man, so recently, right under her eyes. He looked back at her, meeting her gaze.

'Of course I didn't do anything of the sort,' he said quietly. 'Of course I wouldn't. I wouldn't push the *farang* in.' And then he smiled. He had acquired Thai ways – he smiled – and she saw immediately what it was. The wrong sort of smile.

LIVING EVERY SECOND

TRACY EDWARDS

'Tracy, Tracy, wake up.'

'What?'

I opened my eyes and looked up into the smiling face of Helena. She held a bowl and a spoon. 'I've brought you some dinner, I didn't think you'd be able to make it to the galley.'

I hadn't eaten since the accident because the painkillers made me feel nauseous.

'Adrienne is doing the cooking. She's wearing her survival suit just in case the pasta decides to leap up and attack her.'

I wanted to laugh but knew it would hurt. Helena helped me sit up. I glanced at the numbers above the chart table. The wind was a steady 50 knots.

'The waves are getting better,' said Helena. 'Adrienne thinks we might be over the worst of it.'

I drifted off to sleep again. At some point Adrienne came back from the galley. She sat at the chart table and began calling up the latest satellite weather maps. Her face had taken on the green glow of the navigation instruments.

'I reckon we should be able to gybe back in another

couple or hours,' she said, showing me the latest map.

'What speed are we doing?'

She glanced at the dials. 'We're keeping it down to 15 knots most of the time. Occasionally we're surfing at 27.'

There was a movement to the left and behind me Miki appeared in her survival suit, looking like an astronaut. I could only see her eyes behind the mask, but they were clearly tired and fraught.

For the next few hours I drifted in and out of sleep, unable to move. Each time the boat smashed into a wave, the muscles down the left side of my spine contracted and I groaned.

Adrienne woke after two hours and checked the messages. I watched her silently and realised how much weight she'd lost. Just after noon GMT, Lee advised us that we could turn back on to our favoured gybe. We had to wait another two hours between squalls before we could change direction.

We had never gybed in 44 knots of wind. Everybody was needed on deck, except the cripple in her bunk.

'Okay, let's do it,' said Miki.

As the boat shifted downwind, Helena winched in the main until the boom was directly over the cockpit. As one side of the boat released the sheets, the other side was winding them on. The main swung from starboard to port and the wind filled the sail. There was a tremendous sense of achievement amongst the crew. After being hammered for so long, we had proved our resilience. We were back in the race.

The ride felt a lot easier with the wind behind us. Occasionally, the 'big cat' would take off and surf, but it wasn't happening so often.

I drifted in and out of sleep, fuzzy with painkillers.

Is this what you wanted, Tracy? I asked myself silently. Is this what you expected? Did you underestimate the challenge?

I found the answers: No. We're still here, aren't we? We're in the race.

A lot of the newspapers and yachting correspondents who had written us off at the start, or hadn't bothered reporting our progress, had changed their minds over the previous few weeks. We were being taken seriously. Survive until the Horn and then we'll come storming home. That was the goal.

At some point, Miki and Emma W. came down to talk to Adrienne and ask about the forecast.

'Can we put some more sail up?' Emma asked.

Adrienne nodded. 'We've been frightened but let's not let that affect us.'

I worried about putting up too much sail too soon. We all had a strong desire to grab back the lost miles, but that shouldn't override other considerations. There was still a lot of breeze and seas were very rough. 'I don't want you taking reefs out too early. Be sensible,' I said. The reefs had lessened the amount of sail we had aloft. I didn't want us rushing to put it back up again while the seas and winds were still too heavy.

Some time later I woke again to the sound of heavy

boots clattering over the God Pod and winches that cranked and echoed through the fibreglass.

'What's happening?'

'We're shaking out another reef,' said Adrienne.

I looked at the numbers. The wind had settled a little, but the seas were still horrible. Everything is relative, of course. Having encountered 50-foot waves, anything less than 40 feet seemed positively benign.

The barometer had risen to 1005 and we were heading slightly east-sou'east at 20 knots. We hoped to gybe between 53°S and 54°S for the next few days, before diving south to round Cape Horn.

For the umpteenth time I wondered if we were pushing the boat too hard. How did I answer a question like that? This whole challenge had been about discovering our limits and pushing back the boundaries of fear. It had never been our intention to just get round the course – we set out to beat the record. To do that meant racing on the edge. It also meant injuries to the crew and damage to the boat.

We were 725 miles behind *Sport Elec*. Adrienne still believed we could catch them by Cape Horn. I thought we could narrow the gap to a day's sailing.

Six hours before dawn, we were heading due east with a boat speed of 18 to 20 knots – very fast for the conditions. Sharon had the wheel and Miki gave her constant advice on how to steer through the waves.

Sensing that there was something behind her, Sharon glanced over her left shoulder. A rogue wave with a face that was almost vertical came out of the darkness. Later,

Sharon said it reached more than halfway up the mast, which made it over 50 feet.

She had time to utter, 'What do I —?' before the wall of water lifted the catamaran like a child's bath toy, balancing her on the edge of the tub. The bows tipped forward and we dropped into the mire. Surfing at more than 30 knots, Sharon tried desperately to pull away but there was too much momentum. We hurtled into the trough and caught up with the wave in front. Both bows speared into water.

My feet struck the bulkhead at the end of my bunk. The stern lifted as the freak wave caught up with us. Within a split second, the catamaran was standing on its nose. I looked across at Adrienne, who had just crawled into her bunk. The look in her eyes said: We're going over.

Crouched at the end of my bunk, I could feel the 'big cat' sliding and trying desperately to come back. It didn't want to go over. Gravity fought against the pressure of water and wind.

My back didn't hurt. I was too terrified.

Sharon had been thrown against the wheel and then past it, landing in the well alongside Miki and Fred.

For those few seconds the clock stopped. How ironic! All through the voyage I had been trying to hold back time and finally it had happened.

Why now? I wanted to cry. We didn't deserve this fate. We had sailed too well to finish our race ignominiously upside down and fighting for our lives.

The 'big cat' fought hard to come back. Ironically, the

same wave that almost pushed us over now rolled underneath and brought the bows back up. The hull settled in the trough and the wind filled the sails with a suddenness that put more strain on the rigging.

Ten or fifteen seconds passed, perhaps longer. I gingerly tried to crawl out of my bunk. Everything not tied down or lodged securely had become debris. Adrienne's and my foul weather gear sloshed in water on the God Pod floor, along with flares, the spare safety harnesses and a laptop. The chart table was strewn with nav books, charts, pencils and emails.

I surveyed the damage as Adrienne tried to clean up. Above us, we heard the creaking and groaning of carbon fibre grating against itself.

Miki appeared at the door. 'The rig's coming down. It's coming down now.' She sounded so calm and matter-of-fact.

My brain screamed a single word, over and over. *No, no, no, no, no, no . . .*

I looked at Adrienne. 'Oh, my God, the record.'

'Sod the record! We're 2,000 miles from anywhere.'

'Send a mayday,' I said, struggling to pull my foul weather gear over my head and shoulders. Miki had already gone back on deck.

My first priority was to send a distress signal and let somebody know our location in case we had to abandon ship. Adrienne hit a 'distress' key on the laptop, which sent an automatic message to the search and rescue service in Falmouth, England. The duty officer would see the signal flash on screen giving the boat's name and position.

Our computer program immediately gave us a list of options, such as sinking, disabled or man overboard. Adrienne ran through them quickly and typed: '*Royal & SunAlliance*. 92-foot catamaran. Lost rig. Position 52° 44S and 129° 49W. Disabled. Will advise if need help. Please stand by.'

Miki yelled from above. 'The boom is over the port hull, the girls won't be able to get out.'

I picked up the phone linking the hulls.

Emma W. answered. 'What was that?'

'That mast has come down. You won't be able to get out of the hatch. Don't panic. Don't bother to get dressed, just grab your clothes. We don't know if the hull has been damaged. We're going to move the mainsail. I want you to climb out and come to the God Pod. You can get dressed here.'

Miki banged three times to wake Miranda, Hannah and Emma R. in the starboard hull. They gathered in the cockpit, wide-eyed with fear and still fastening their drysuits.

I scrambled on deck wearing just my mid-layers. My back no longer hurt – pure adrenalin had neutralised the pain. I couldn't see a thing. The deck lights had come down with the mast. Miki shone a torch over the devastation. It revealed itself a small piece at a time.

The mast had crumpled rather than fallen over. Initially, it had broken near the top at the third spreader. Miki had seen it break again at the second spreader and then at the first before it crumpled over the port side.

As I surveyed the damage, I felt as though my insides

were being cut open and torn out. A wave slammed into the starboard hull and exploded over the cockpit and netting. I blinked away salt water that might have been tears.

Sharon was distraught. 'We just came down the wave. I couldn't get off. I did everything I could to get off . . . we had nowhere to go . . .'

'It's okay, Sharon. It's not your fault.'

'. . . and then the mast just came down. I have never ever willed something to stay up there so much in my life. "No, no, don't fall down." It was falling. Then it broke again. "No, no, you don't want to do that." And then it broke at the base. Oh, my God.'

It wasn't Sharon's fault, or anyone else's. Ultimately, the responsibility rested with me.

'We have to get the girls out,' said Miki, struggling to be heard above the wind. The bottom section of the mast lay across the netting. The boom and mainsail covered the port hatch.

'Hannah, grab a hacksaw in case we have to cut anything away.'

Using torches they picked their way through the debris and began lifting the boom. I went back to join Adrienne, who had been sending messages to search and rescue centres in Chile, New Zealand and Australia. The reality of our plight was clear from the map. We were 2,500 miles from New Zealand, 2,300 miles from Chile and 1,200 miles from Antarctica. We couldn't have chosen a place any further from rescue if we'd tried.

Having been freed, Helena, Sam and Emma W. arrived

in the God Pod still wearing their thermals. Helena hobbled on a badly bruised knee but it had probably saved her life. If she hadn't fallen in the nose-dive, she would have been coming out of the hatch as the rig came down. The boom would have landed on top of her.

Sam was like a rabbit caught in a spotlight. Emma looked at me and I realised that she'd been saying the same thing over and over again: 'Oh, God, the record, the record.'

She put her arms around me. 'We nearly did it, Tracy.'

I almost cracked. I could feel the tears welling in my eyes and a lump at the back of my throat. No, Tracy, hold it together. Don't lost it. I had to be cool-headed; totally unfazed.

The heavy seas were bashing the rigging against the port hull. It might already have been holed. The catamaran wasn't likely to sink unless the watertight compartments had been breached.

Miki controlled things on deck. I had complete faith in her. She had been dismasted twice before and each time the crew had managed to put up a jury rig and sail to safety. I could hear her shouting instructions from the cockpit. I helped Sam get dressed.

'Are they coming to get us?' she asked.

'Yes, if we need them.'

'Is it going to be okay?'

'Absolutely.'

I sent a single-line message to race headquarters in Hamble: 'Charlotte, we have lost our rig. We are sorting it out at this stage. We are in distress. The position is 52° 44S and 129° 51W.'

Adrienne maintained contact with maritime rescue centres in Australia, Chile and New Zealand. If we discovered a breach in the port hull, we'd need their help quickly. The same was true if we couldn't rig a makeshift sail.

Miki and Hannah swung into the nav station. Both were breathing hard and dripping wet. They braced themselves against the bulkheads near the hatchway as the boat pitched and rolled.

'The mast is broken in three places and hanging over the port hull,' said Miki. 'The upper two-thirds are in the water. The only thing holding the sections together are torn pieces of mainsail and reefing lines.'

Hannah continued: 'We have water coming into the starboard hull but it doesn't look like a breach. I think a chain plate has been ripped from the deck and water is coming through when waves come over the top.'

'How bad is it?'

'I've told Sharon to turn on the bilge pump,' said Miki.

'Okay, I'll turn on the generator. Is there any sign of damage to the port hull?'

'We don't know yet. We'll have to wait until we cut the rig away.'

'Do it as quickly as you can. You've got to cut away the rigging hanging over the side.'

Hannah said anxiously, 'We must try to save as much as we can. We can use it to make a new mast.'

'Yes, but if it does look like endangering the boat, you have to let it go.'

Both nodded in agreement. I continued: 'We got ourselves

into this situation and it's our responsibility to get ourselves out of it. At the moment we don't need saving, but that could change very quickly.' As if to prove my point, a wave slammed into the bottom of the God Pod and rattled my spine.

'Miki, you're in charge of what everyone does. Hannah, you're in charge of the logistics of getting rid of the mast. I want you to tell Miranda that it's her job to make sure everyone stays on the boat. They won't be able to clip on easily. She won't be able to shine a torch in their eyes. Tell her to do a roll-call every few minutes.'

The entire crew gathered in the cockpit and I caught glimpses of their faces in the torchlight as Miki briefed them. I knew they were all frightened, yet there was a tremendous sense of determination and resolve.

Miki and Hannah began issuing instructions. Tools had to be found. There were hacksaws in each of the hulls and in the God Pod. Wire-cutters and more blades were kept in the forward lockers. Emma W. took a torch and began picking her way through the debris.

Miranda kept watch as the darkness closed behind Emma and all that was visible was the bouncing circle of light in her hand.

'I want some of you to put on life-jackets rather than safety harnesses,' said Miki. 'I don't want you clipping on in case you're attached to something that's going over the side. Miranda, you'll stay in the cockpit and do the roll-calls.'

I could hear their boots on the God Pod roof as they

began cutting away the rigging. There are hundreds of yards of wire, ropes, reefing lines and torn cloth – all tangled together and wrapped around the broken mast. It looked as though a massive spider had wrapped its spindly legs around the hulls and tried to wrap us in its web.

Although the catamaran pitched and rolled, the broken mast seemed to act as a sea anchor, holding us solid in the water. Even without a sail we *were* doing 2 knots – what an unbelievable boat, she just wouldn't give up!

Waves crashed over the starboard hull and exploded up through the netting with even more force than before. Instead of coming from forward to back, as they did when we were moving, the waves erupted straight up, lifting girls clear off the netting.

The next four hours passed in a blur of hacksaws and wire-cutters. Miki and Hannah tried to bring in the second section of mast lying nearest the port hull but it broke and had to be cut away. The girls worked without a break.

At one stage, I came on deck to find Emma R. using a hacksaw blade with her bare hands because she couldn't find the handle.

As the first tinges of grey light emerged on the eastern horizon, the full scale of the devastation emerged. My heart felt ready to break. Debris littered the decks and netting. Padeyes and chain plates had been ripped out, stanchions had caved in, cracks had opened, ropes and torn sails dragged in the water. A thoroughbred racing catamaran had become little more than a floating platform.

I came on deck as the last of the rig was cut away. Miki sawed through the carbon fibre on the middle section of the mast. The girls all stood and watched in silence as she cut through the final half-inch. As it separated, the rig and mainsail slid over the side and disappeared. I felt as though I had watched the body of a friend being buried at sea.

We had managed to save 21 feet of mast. It now lay across the netting alongside the boom. I still didn't know if we could put it back up, or if it would disintegrate under the weight of a makeshift sail.

Hannah leaned over the port hull, examining it for damage. It appeared to be intact, although some of the padeyes had ripped out of the deck, creating small holes.

It was now fully light. The girls had been working solidly for six hours.

'Right, everybody in the God Pod,' I said.

People sat where they could find space and a few had to stay outside and huddle near the hatch. Sam had gone to make tea for everybody. Emma R. asked, 'Do you think we can break into the Sunday cake?'

'Emma, this is probably just the occasion to break into the Sunday cake.'

'Brilliant.'

She dashed across to the galley and returned with the fruit cake and a knife. As she cut slices and handed them out, I struggled to get my head around the bizarre sight of eleven women having a tea party in the middle of the Southern Ocean on a crippled yacht.

I looked at the faces around me. Miranda and Sharon

were wide-eyed, as if almost in shock. Miki looked exhausted, but tried to make light of it. Sam had grown very quiet, which worried me a little. Little Emma looked to be almost in denial, the way she bounced and laughed, handing out pieces of cake. It was if she'd said: I can't deal with this, so I'll pretend it hasn't happened.

Hannah seemed angry and aggressive. I think she was pissed off at having endured weeks of misery only to discover that we weren't going to get all the way round.

Adrienne had been quite boisterous and upbeat. Although I didn't realise it at the time, I think she concentrated on me during those first few hours because she was so worried about me.

'Right, let's get down to business,' I said. 'I'm putting Hannah in charge of putting the mast back up. I'm not asking you if it can be done, Hannah, because it *has* to be done. I don't care what it looks like, as long as it works.

'Miki, I want you to help Hannah and give everybody their tasks. Sharon, you'll have to sew us some new sails. Adrienne will keep the emergency services updated and I'll stay in touch with the office and do any other comms.'

One of the reasons I had chosen Hannah for the voyage was her ability as a 'boat bodger'. Now she had her ultimate challenge – she had to make us a new mast.

For the next five hours the girls worked tirelessly. Hannah cut wooden spars from spare timber in the cockpit. These fitted inside the hollow top of the mast, bracing the outer edges apart so it wouldn't collapse. Four support cables were attached which we hoped would hold the mast in place once we pulled it upright.

There were two blocks at the front and one at the back, with a halyard going up and down.

The most difficult task lay ahead: how to lift the truncated mast into place.

Eleven hours after the disaster, we were ready to try. Miki and Hannah had rigged up a pulley system to hoist it upright. There were two lines leading through blocks back to the cockpit winches and two lines that were to be pulled by hand. Another line ran forward through a block and then came back to one of the winches.

With everyone in position, Hannah gave the orders:

'Sam, wind on a bit more . . . Not too quickly, Sharon . . . Steady . . . steady . . . keep it coming . . . '

The catamaran bucked and rocked in the swell, making the job more difficult. As the mast edged upwards, Hannah tried to make sure it was straight.

'Okay, set it down.' Four people gripped the base of the mast and made small adjustments as it slid home. As the lines were cleated off, nobody felt like cheering. We didn't have the energy.

Sharon had prepared the storm jib as our first sail. With only 21 feet of mast, we would have to raise it sideways, with the corner that was normally sheeted in becoming the top. Clipping it to the halyard, it took her less than two seconds to hoist it aloft. Hannah sheeted it off and it bulged with the breeze. Ropes tightened on the winches and the new support lines creaked.

We were off again, with Miki at the wheel.

Adrienne asked the search and rescue service to stand down. We would give them positional reports every six hours. Meanwhile, I sent a message to Charlotte:

> *We are doing nine knots towards Chile. We will just head in the general direction of the coast at 50°S until we have some information on where to go.*
>
> *It is really difficult trying not to show how much my heart is breaking at the moment and to keep people's spirits up at the same time. Adrienne is being great and mopping up the tears so we don't drown.*
>
> *Lots of love and thoughts, Tracy.*

Nobody underestimated the danger we still faced. We were deep into the Southern Ocean on a crippled yacht, directly in the path of two more fronts. George and Lee wanted us to get further north because the lows would catch and pass us quickly. The next would arrive within 48 hours, bringing forecast winds of up to 45 knots. I knew the jury rig wouldn't stand up to a severe storm.

Helena and Hannah began preparing the boat for the rougher weather, checking the drogues, tweaking the jury rig and filling any holes on deck with epoxy. Sharon and Fred worked for hours in the dungeon to turn the staysail into a main.

In London, a media release was drafted to break the news. As I read the statement, I seemed almost detached.

So much had happened in the previous eighteen hours that I hadn't thought about the ramifications of failure. Here it was, set out for me; summed up in a few paragraphs:

Royal & SunAlliance, the 92ft catamaran skippered by Tracy Edwards with an all-female crew of ten, has been forced to abandon its attempts on the Round the World non-stop record for the Trophée Jules Verne.

In pitch darkness at 0850 GMT this morning, on her forty-third day at sea having covered approximately 15,200 miles since setting off from Ushant, north-west France on 3rd February, disaster struck Royal & SunAlliance. In 40-feet seas and winds gusting from 30 to 50 knots, a huge wave came up behind them, lifting the stern and burying both bows in the wave ahead bringing the boat to a shuddering halt. About five minutes later, creaking could be heard from the top of the mast and the whole thing just crumpled over the port side and broke up as it hit the hull.

The all-female crew, who are safe and well, are getting to grips with the new challenge of making the boat sailable and heading for land, some 2,000 miles away in South America. There is no possibility of pursuing the record.

At the time of the disaster, the boat had covered about 350 miles in the last twenty-four hours, and had averaged 435 miles a day over the last nine days in the relentless pursuit of the record of 71 days, 14 hours, 22 minutes and 8 seconds set last year by Frenchman Olivier de Kersauson.

Speaking from the boat, Tracy Edwards said: 'We are disappointed beyond belief as we were so close to getting to Cape Horn in such good time against the record. Words cannot describe how we feel at the moment although the girls are once again pulling on their reserves of strength to get through this.'

These words didn't even come close to conveying how I really felt. I was devastated. That night I cried silently, overcome by a sense of having sacrificed four years of my life for nothing. I woke after six hours, hollow-eyed and echoing inside. I didn't want to speak to anyone or hear words of comfort.

It was as though someone had died and nobody knew what to say. All of the girls were grieving; unable to talk about how they felt because the shared sadness would have been overwhelming. I was grateful for the fact that nobody mentioned what happened, but I knew I couldn't hide for ever. Eventually, I would have to put on my bravest face and confront reality.

At first light, Emma R. began filming some reaction scenes for the BBC documentary. I didn't know if there'd still be one.

'I really can't believe this has happened,' I said. 'It wasn't meant to. We have all been to the finish so many times in our minds. We were so frigging close. We were going to be a day behind Olivier at Cape Horn and we were going to burn him off on the way home. We were going to do it. I just can't believe it.'

Next she interviewed Adrienne who, true to form, said: 'We could have dithered around and made it, coming in behind Olivier but ahead of where people expected. Instead, we took it as a serious record attempt and sailed the boat like it should be sailed. We were up to it, but the rig wasn't .'

I woke in the milky grey light of the God Pod. Adrienne's bunk was empty. A sound of hammering puzzled me and then I felt my chest. I took a deep breath and tried to slow my heart.

Had it all been a dream?

One glance at the blank navigation screens removed any doubt.

That's it for me, I thought. I'm never setting foot on a boat again. I don't want to break records. I don't want to go sailing. I want to curl up in bed and never show my face again. From now on if I need a challenge I'll take up crocheting.

I had been wrong to do this. I had set myself too big a task; bitten off more than I could chew. And all those doubters would now be crowing, 'I told you so.'

They were right. I was wrong.

Tilting my head I saw Sam's legs at the wheel and could hear Sharon whispering. I wanted to hear her voice boom, but she had lost her Kiwi bluster and brightness. I wanted to hear Sam laugh and Helena tell a rude joke in her matter-of-fact accent. I wanted to hear Fred mix up her English words and Emma say, 'Oops' when she split something in the galley.

Most of all, I wanted to turn back the clock and start again. Not just 24 hours – I couldn't have stopped that mast coming down – but four years. I wanted to recreate that moment when the idea of winning the Jules Verne trophy first came to me. Then I would bury it so deeply that it never occurred to me again.

The shock hadn't dissipated. It had settled on the boat like suffocating fog. The 2,000 miles to Chile stretched in front of us like a prison sentence. We were in the middle of nowhere on a floating platform with a 21-foot pole sticking up from the middle. Our once beautiful sails were cut up and hanging limply from the top.

There was not a breath of wind yet still the 'big cat' clawed her way eastwards at 5 knots. She had brought us through the most dangerous ocean in the world, battling conditions known only to a few sailors. Only when the sea picked her up and dashed her down did she finally surrender.

I had changed the watch system because we didn't need three girls on deck any more. From now on we'd sail in pairs, working three hours on and nine hours off. This gave everybody a chance to recuperate.

Adrienne and I barely slept during those few days because important decisions still had to be made. The girls seemed to hide away, cocooned in their sleeping bags. Nobody wanted to talk.

By Friday they began to spend less time sleeping. They emerged on deck or gathered in the God Pod to read their mail. Nobody discussed the race or the record. Occasionally, I felt an arm around my shoulders. 'Are you okay?'

'Yeah. Fine.'

As the girls started taking over, Adrienne and I retreated and slept.

I thought back to 1990 when *Maiden* sailed into Southampton at the end of the Whitbread. An armada of yachts, power boats and dinghies came out to meet us for the final three miles. I had never been so proud or so moved.

From feeling on top of the world I now scrabbled on the floor on my hands and knees. One minute I was right up there, a success story, the next minute I was nothing. The disappointment was almost suffocating. I had failed. I had let my family, friends and supporters down.

That night as I collected the emails, I found a message from Ed. He had sent me another poem by one of my favourite writers, Robert Service. It was a lovely gesture and very moving. Maybe Ed had more feminine qualities than I had first suspected.

THE QUITTER

When you're lost in the Wild, and you're scared as a child,
  And Death looks you bang in the eye,
And you're sore as a boil, it's according to Hoyle
  To cock your revolver and . . . die.
But the Code of a Man says: 'Fight all you can,'
  And self-dissolution is barred.
In hunger and woe, oh, it's easy to blow . . .
  It's the hell-served-for-breakfast that's hard.

'You're sick of the game!' Well, now that's a shame.
　　You're young and you're brave and you're bright.
'You've had a raw deal!' I know – but don't squeal,
　　Buck up, do your damnedest, and fight.
It's the plugging away that will win you the day,
　　So don't be a piker, old pard!
Just draw on your grit; it's so easy to quit.
　　It's the keeping-your-chin-up that's hard.

It's easy to cry that you're beaten – and die;
　　It's easy to crawfish and crawl;
But to fight and to fight when hope's out of sight –
　　Why that's the best game of them all!
And though you come out of each gruelling bout
　　All broken and beaten and scarred,
Just have one more try – it's dead easy to die,
　　It's the keeping-on-living that's hard.

FAITH AND HOPE FLY SOUTH

JOANNE HARRIS

How NICE OF YOU TO take the trouble. It isn't everyone who would give up their time to listen to two old biddies with nothing much to do with themselves but talk. Still, there's always something going on here at the Meadowbank Home; some domestic drama, some everyday farce. I tell you, some days the Meadowbank Home is just like the West End, as I often tell my son Tom when he calls in on his weekly dash to somewhere else, bearing petrol-station flowers (usually chrysanths, which last a long time, more's the pity), and stirring tales of the World Outside.

Well, no, not really – I made that last bit up. Tom's conversation tends to be rather like his flowers: sensible, unimaginative and bland. But he does come, bless him, which is more than you could say for most of them, with their soap-opera lives and their executive posts and their touching belief that life stops at sixty (or should), with all of those unsightly, worrying creases neatly tucked away. Hope and I know better.

You know Hope, of course. Being blind, I think she appreciates your visits even more than I do; they try to find things to entertain us, but when you've been a professor at Cambridge, with theatres and cocktail parties and May Balls and Christmas concerts at King's, you never really learn to appreciate those Tuesday-night bingo games. On the other hand, you do learn to appreciate small pleasures (small pleasures being by far the commonest) because, as some French friend of Hope's used to say, one can imagine even Sisyphus happy. (Sisyphus, in case you don't know, was the fellow doomed by the gods to roll a rock up a hill for ever.) I'm not an intellectual, like Hope, but I think I see what he means. He's saying there's nothing you can't get used to – given time.

Of course, in a place like this, there are always your malcontents. There's Polish John, whose name no one can ever pronounce, who never has a good word to say to any of us. Or Mr Braun, who has quite a sense of humour in spite of being a German, but who gets very depressed when they show war films on TV. Or Mrs Swathen, whom everybody envies because her son and his family take her out every single week, who has grandchildren who visit her and a sweet-faced daughter-in-law who brings her presents; but Mrs Swathen gripes and moans continually because she is bored, and the children don't come often enough, and her bowels are bad, and the food is dreadful, and no one knows what she has to suffer. Mrs Swathen is the only person (except for Lorraine, the new nurse) who has ever made Hope lose her temper. Still, we manage, Hope and I. Like Sara in *A Little Princess* (a book Hope loved as a child and I re-read to her just last month when we finished *Lolita*), we try not to let the Mrs Swathens of this world poison our lives. We take our pleasures where we can. We try to behave like princesses, even if we are not.

Of course, there are exceptions. This week, for example, this August 10th, on the occasion of the Meadowbank Home's annual day trip to the sea. Every year in August we go, all of us packed into a fat orange coach with blankets and picnics and flasks of milky tea and the Meadowbank nurses – cheery or harassed, according to type – on what Hope calls the Incontinence Express to Blackpool.

I've always liked Blackpool. We used to go there every year, you know, when Tom was little, and I remember watching him playing in the rock pools while Peter lay asleep on the warm grey sand and the waves sighed in and out on the shingle. In those days it was our place; we had our regular guesthouse, where everyone remembered us, and Mrs Neames made bacon and eggs for breakfast and always cooed over how much Tom had grown. We had our regular teashop, too, where we went for hot chocolate after we'd gone swimming in the cold sea, and our chip shop, the Happy Haddock, where we always went for lunch. Perhaps that's why I still love it now: the long beach; the parade of shops; the pier; the waterfront where the big waves crash over the road at high tide. Hope loves it by default; you'd think Blackpool would be a bit of a climbdown for her, after holidays on the Riviera, but Hope would never say so, and looks forward to our trips, I think, with as much enthusiasm and excitement as I do myself –

which made it all the harder to take when Lorraine told us that this year we couldn't go.

Lorraine is our newest nurse, a poison blonde with pencilled lips and a smell of Silk Cut and Juicy Fruit gum. She replaces Kelly, who was dim but innocuous, and she is a great favourite of Maureen, the general manager. Lorraine, too, has her favourites, among whom Hope and I do not count, and when Maureen is away (which is about once a week), she holds court in the Residents' Lounge, drinking tea, eating digestive biscuits and stirring up unrest. Mrs Swathen, a great admirer of hers, says that Lorraine is the only really sensible person at the Meadowbank Home, although Hope and I have noticed that their conversation revolves principally around Mrs Swathen's undeserving son, and how much he is to inherit when Mrs Swathen dies. Far too much, or so I understand – with the result that after only a couple of months here, Lorraine has already managed to convince Mrs Swathen that she is badly neglected.

'Ambulance-chaser,' says Hope in disgust. You get them from time to time in places like this; insinuating girls like Lorraine, flattering the malcontents, spreading their poison. And poison is addictive; in time people come to depend on that poison, as they do on those poisonous reality shows Lorraine enjoys so much. Little pleasures fade, and one comes to realise that there are greater pleasures to be had in self-pity, and complaint, and viciousness towards one's fellow residents. That's Lorraine; and although Maureen is no Samaritan, with her Father Christmas jollity and vacuum salesman's smile she is infinitely better than Lorraine, who thinks that Hope and I are too clever by half, and who tries in her underhand way to rob us of every small pleasure we still have left.

Our trip to Blackpool, for instance.

Let me explain. A few months ago, Hope and I escaped from the home – a day trip to London, that's all, but to the Meadowbank staff it might as well have been a jailbreak. That was just before Maureen's time – Lorraine's too – but I can tell that the thought of such a breakout appals her. Lorraine is equally appalled – for a different reason – and often speaks to us in the syrupy tones of a cross nursery teacher, explaining how *naughty* it was of us to run away, how worried everyone was on our behalf, and how it serves us right that we missed the chance to sign up for the Blackpool trip this August, and must now stay behind with Chris, the orderly, and Sad Harry, the emergency nurse.

Sign up, my foot. We never used to have to sign up for our day trips. With Maureen in charge, however, things have changed; Health and Safety have got involved; there is insurance to consider, permission slips to sign and a whole administrative procedure to put into place before even the shortest excursion can be considered.

'I'm sorry, girls, but you had your chance,' said Lorraine virtuously. 'Rules are rules, and *surely* you don't expect Maureen to make an *exception* for you.'

I have to say I don't much like the idea of Tom having to sign a slip – it reminds me so much of the times when he used to bring those forms home from grammar school, wanting permission to go on trips to France, or even skiing in Italy; trips we could barely afford but which we paid for anyway because Tom was a good boy, Tom was going to do well, and Peter and I didn't want to show him up in front of his friends. Now, of course, Tom holidays all over the place – New York, Florida, Sydney, Tenerife – though he has yet to invite me on any of his trips. He never had much imagination, you know. He never imagines, poor boy, that I might dream of hurtling down the *piste noire* at Val d'Isère, or being serenaded in Venice, or lounging in a hammock in Hawaii with a Mai Tai in each hand. I suppose he still thinks Blackpool's all I've ever wanted.

As for Hope – well, Hope rarely lets her feelings show. I see them, because I know Hope better than anyone, but I doubt Lorraine got much satisfaction. 'Blackpool?' she said in her snootiest, most dismissive Cambridge voice. 'Not really my cup of tea, Lorraine. We had a villa, you know, in Eze-sur-Mer, on the French Riviera. We went there, the three of us, twice a year, all the time Priss was growing up. It was quiet in those days – not as overrun with film people and celebrities as it is now – but we used to pop down to Cannes from time to time, if there was a party we really wanted to go to. Most of the time, though, we stayed by the pool, or went sailing in Xavier's yacht – he was a friend of Cary Grant's, you know, and on several occasions Cary and I—'

By then, though, I was laughing so much that I almost spilt my tea. 'It's all right,' I said, taking Hope's arm. 'She's gone.'

'Good,' said Hope. 'I hate showing off, but sometimes . . .'

Lorraine was watching us from the far side of the
Residents' Lounge. Her face was a study in pique.
'Sometimes it's worth it,' I said, still grinning. 'If only to
see that woman's face.'

Hope, who couldn't see it, smiled. 'No Blackpool, then,'
she said, pouring tea expertly into one of the Meadowbank
cups. 'Still, there's next year, God willing. Pass me a digestive, Faith, if you would.'

Next year, next year. That's all well and good when
you're twenty-five, but at our age, next year isn't something
that all of us can count on. Hope and I are still all right, not
like Mrs McAllister, who hardly knows what day it is, or Mr
Bannerman, whose lungs are so riddled that he has to have
a machine at night to help him breathe – and who still
smokes like a chimney, foul-mouthed old tosspot that he is,
because in his own words, *who the hell wants to live for ever?*

Besides, I happen to know how much those occasional
day trips mean to Hope. Oh I enjoy them, of course, even
though most of the things I remember so well have gone.
The Happy Haddock is an Irish pub nowadays, and the
guesthouses have all been knocked down to make way for
that new housing estate. Hope, on the other hand, does not
have to bear with these small disappointments. She can
still smell the Blackpool sea, that peculiarly British seaside
smell of tidal mud and petrol, fried fish and suntan oil and
candyfloss and salt. She likes the sound of the waves, the
long crash-hiss of the water on the pebbly shore, the cries

of the children testing the water with their toes. She likes the feel of the sand beneath her feet – in my wheelchair I can't guide her on the soft sand, but Chris always takes her down to the beach – and that half-yielding crunch of shingle before the beach gives way to pebbles. She enjoys the picnic we share – always in the same place, a part of the beach that slopes down a cobbly ramp to give wheelchair access those of us who need it – the thermos of tea, the two neat quarter sandwiches (always the same, barring allergies: one tuna, one egg) and the single pink fairy cake, nine-tenths sugar with a bright red synthetic half-cherry on top, like the ones we used to have for our birthdays when we were girls. She likes to pick up shells on the tideline – big, thick, English shells, flaky and barnacled on the outside, pearly-smooth inside – and line her pockets with worn, round stones.

What she doesn't see, I can always describe to her, although in many ways Hope notices far more than I do myself. It isn't a sixth sense, or anything like that; it's simply that she always makes the most of what she has.

'It'll be fine,' she told me, when I complained once again about being left out. 'We'll manage. Remember Sara.'

Remember Sara. Easily said. But it's the unfairness of it that kept me awake at night; the petty unfairness of it all. *Rules are rules*, Lorraine had said, but we both knew why we were being denied the treat, like children caught smoking behind the sheds. It's about power, like all bullying, and Lorraine, like all bullies, was both weak and addicted to the weakness of others. Of course, we knew better than to show her our disappointment. Cheery Chris saw it – and was angry on our behalf, though there was nothing he could do to help. We never even complained to Maureen – though personally I doubted it would have had any effect. Instead we talked about the Riviera, and the scent of thyme rolling off the hills, and the Mediterranean in shades of miraculous blue, and barbecued mackerel and cocktails by the pool, and girls in itsy-bitsy polka-dot bikinis lounging on the decks of yachts with sails like the wings of impossible birds.

Only Chris knew the truth. Cheery Chris with his one earring and messy hair drawn back in a ponytail. He isn't actually a nurse at all – although he does a nurse's job on less than half the pay – but he's our favourite, the only one who really talks to us like fellow human beings. 'Bad luck, Butch,' was all he said when he heard the news, but there was more real sympathy in the way he said it than in all of Lorraine's syrupy little lectures. 'Looks like you're stuck with me, then,' he said, grinning. 'Seems like I'm not wanted, either.'

That made me smile, too. Lorraine doesn't like Chris, whom all the residents like even though he isn't a proper nurse, who calls me Butch and Hope Sundance, and who shows none of the proper respect and deference to his superiors that you might expect from someone in his position.

'We'll have an old sing-song, just the three of us, eh?'

Chris often sings to us when the boss is out of earshot:

rock ballads, tunes from the musicals and old vaudeville songs he learned from his gran. He has quite a nice voice and he knows all the old hits, and he has been known to waltz me about in my wheelchair so that I feel quite dizzy with laughter; although in all his silly nonsense I have never caught a glimpse of the kind of condescension you see in people like Maureen or Lorraine.

'Thank you, Christopher, that would be lovely,' said Hope with a smile, and Chris went away feeling he'd cheered us up a little. I knew better, though. Hope would never say it, but I knew her disappointment. It wasn't the Incontinence Express and the flasks of lukewarm tea, it wasn't the single fairy cake, it wasn't the feel of sand between her bare toes or the smell of salt coming off the water. It wasn't even the hurt of being talked down to as if we were children, or the knowledge that we were being left out. It was the illusion of freedom, the promise of parole, the smell of the air, the sound of young people going about their business on an ordinary summer's day. Meadowbank air has a certain smell: of floral air-freshener, school cabbage and the bland, powdery smell that comes off old people living in close proximity to one other. Hope wears Chanel No. 5 every day because that way, she says, she can at least avoid *smelling* like an old woman. I know exactly how she feels.

And so when the day came it was with a secret sense of desolation that we watched them go, although we would rather have died than show it. One by one, the residents shook out their summer coats (Meadowbank chic dictates that coats, hats, scarves and, sometimes, gloves *must* be worn on even the hottest day) and collected bags, hankies, umbrellas, dentures and a variety of other items indispensable for a day at the sea.

Mrs Swathen gave me a look as she picked up her handbag. 'They're saying it's twenty-five degrees by the coast today,' she said. 'Just like the Med, today, they're saying.'

'How nice,' said Hope. 'But Faith and I don't like it when it's too hot. I think we'll just stay in and watch TV.'

Mrs Swathen, who would normally have spent all afternoon watching *Jerry Springer* and getting more and more indignant about it, ground her teeth. 'Please yourselves,' she said, and stalked off towards the coach.

Polish John watched her go. 'Don't listen to her,' he said. 'It will rain again. I know it will rain. It always rains when we go to the sea. I myself do not enjoy the sea, but anything is better than another day in this Auschwitz, no?'

Mr Braun, who was passing, turned round at that. He is a small, neat, bald man who walks with a stick and likes to bait Polish John. 'You ignorant,' he said fiercely. 'Don't you know my father *died* at Auschwitz?'

Well, that fairly stumped Polish John. It was the first we'd heard of it, too, and we all stared at Mr Braun, wondering if he'd suddenly gone strange, like Mrs McAllister.

Mr Braun nodded. 'Yes,' he said. 'He got drunk one night and fell out of the guard tower.' And then he was off, leaving Hope and I laughing fit to burst and Polish John frothing (not for the first time) with indignation in his wake.

'Well, if that's the level of camaraderie we can expect on this trip,' I said, 'then I for one can bear to give it a miss.'

'I agree,' said Hope. 'Imagine being stuck in a coach for two hours with those two – and Maureen – and Lorraine – and Mrs Swathen. I'm beginning to believe Sartre was right when he said, *Hell is other people*.'

Sometimes Hope forgets that I'm not familiar with these French colleagues of hers. Still, that was a good one. But as the party got ready to leave at last, I felt that sense of desolation return. The orange coach opened its doors and the staff nurses got on board, little Helen, cross Claire, then Lorraine, looking pleased with herself (as well she might), and finally fat Maureen, swollen with jollity, baying, 'Isn't this *fun*! Isn't this *fun*!' as she shooed the last of the residents inside. At the back window, Mrs McAllister, small, shrivelled and bright-eyed, was piping, 'Goodbye! Goodbye!' in her thin, excited voice. I suppose she thought she was going home again. Mrs McAllister always thinks she's going home. Perhaps that was why she seemed to be wearing all of her wardrobe that day – I could see at least three coats, a tartan, a brown and a light blue summer raincoat, pockets bulging with extra pairs of shoes. That made me laugh, but as the coach finally pulled out of the drive, making the gravel *hishhh* under its wheels like breakers on shingle, I felt tears come to my eyes, and I knew Hope was feeling just the same.

'Remember Sara,' I muttered, but this time I knew that *A Little Princess* wasn't going to help. A cup of tea might not help either, but I poured one anyway, from the urn on the sideboard, and wheeled my chair to the bay so that I could look out of the window.

It was going to be a long day.

My tea tasted of fish. It often does when it has stood for too long, and I put it aside. Hope came to sit next to me, using the ramps to feel her way forward, and she sat there quietly for a while, drinking the fishy tea and feeling the morning sun on her face.

'Well, Faith. At least we're alone,' she said at last.

That was true. The Meadowbank Home doesn't have a hospital wing, and anyone needing day-to-day medical help has to go to All Saints' down the road. I went there once when I had my bout of bronchitis, and Mr Bannerman goes there every week for his check-ups. But today even Mr Bannerman had gone to the sea, and we were alone with Denise, the receptionist, Sad Harry, the emergency nurse, and Chris, who had been given so many jobs to do in Maureen's absence (washing windows, changing light bulbs, hoeing flowerbeds) that I doubted if we'd see him at all.

For most of the morning I was proved right. Tea came and went, then lunch (cottage pie), which we picked at without much appetite. Time passes at a different rate here, but even so it seemed unbearably slow. Usually there's a film on TV in the afternoon, but that day there wasn't; just a dull procession of people like Mrs Swathen complaining about their relatives. Hope tried her best, but by two o'clock her conversation had dried up altogether and we just sat there like bookends, wishing it was over, waiting for the sound of the coach on the gravel. Even then, I knew, it wouldn't be over. Even then we would have to bear with their talk of what they had seen, what they had done. Days out are rare at Meadowbank; this one might give them six months' worth of gossip, six months of *do-you-remember-that-time-in-Blackpool*, so that I felt almost sick at the thought of it. Hope felt it, too; in fact, Hope feels it all the time to some extent – after all, she has to deal with a fair amount of that kind of thing, those thoughtless, well-meaning *if-only-you-could-have-seen-it* comments that only serve to remind her that she is blind.

I looked at her then, and saw the expression on her face. At first I thought she'd been crying, but Hope never cries. I did, though. I made no sound, but Hope took my hand anyway, and I thought maybe I'd been wrong about that sixth sense. We sat there for a long time – for me, anyway – until I couldn't hold it any longer and had to call Sad Harry to take me to the bathroom.

I got back to the Residents' Lounge to find Chris waiting for me. 'Hey, Butch,' he said, grinning, and all at once I felt much better. There's something about Chris that does that, a kind of nonsense that pulls you along like a crazy dance. When I was a girl I used to ride the waltzers at the fair, spinning round and round in a two-seater chair shaped like a giant teacup and laughing breathlessly all the time. Chris makes me feel like that sometimes. I suppose it's because he's young – although Tom never made me feel like that, not even when he was twenty.

'Have you finished your work?' I asked, knowing that

Chris works very hard, but hoping that he might spare us a few minutes, just this once.

'I'm all yours, sweetheart,' he said, grinning, and spun me round in my wheelchair, causing Harry to protest. 'In fact, I brought you a few things.' He waved Harry away with an airy hand. 'Secret things, Harry, so scat.'

Sad Harry huffed and rolled his eyes. He's not a bad fellow – not so cheery as Chris, but not half as bad as Lorraine – and I saw his grin as he closed the door.

'Secret things?' said Hope with a smile.

'You betcha. Cop a look at these, for a start.' And he dropped a pile of glossy magazine brochures into my lap. The Algarve, the West Indies, the Riviera, the Cook Islands all spilled out across my knees; lagoons, Easter-lily beaches, yachts, spas, wooden platters of tropical fruits piled high with pineapples, coconuts, mango, papaya.

When it comes to reading, Hope likes books and I have always had a soft spot for magazines. The glossier the better: couture and garden parties, city breaks and designer shoes. I gave a little squeak as I saw the brochures, and Chris laughed.

'That's not all,' he said. 'Close your eyes.'

'What?'

'Close your eyes. Both of you. And don't open them until I say so.'

So we did, feeling like children, but in a good way this time. For several minutes Chris moved around us, and I could hear him picking things up and putting things down. A match flared; there came a chink of glass, then a rustle of paper, then a number of clicks and rattles that I did not recognise. Finally I felt him pulling my chair backwards into the window bay; a second later there came the sound of him dragging Hope's armchair alongside. Warmth on my hair; soft air from the open window; outside a distant drone of bees.

'Okay, ladies,' said Chris. 'Off we go.'

We were sitting in the bay with our backs to the window. Late afternoon sunlight illuminated the room, making the Residents' Lounge into a magic-lantern show. I turned my head and saw that Chris had hung several of the crystal pendants from the hall chandelier in the bay, so that prisms of coloured light danced across the flock wallpaper. Several posters had been tacked to the walls (quite contravening Meadowbank regulations): white houses under a purple sky; islands seen from the air like flamenco dancers shaking their skirts; bare-chested, beautiful young men standing hip-deep among green vines. I laughed aloud at the sheer absurdity; and saw that he had lit four glass-covered candles on the sideboard (another Meadowbank rule broken). On them I could read a foreign word – *Diptyque* – that I did not recognise. From them a faint scent diffused.

'It's thyme, isn't it?' said Hope beside me. 'Wild purple thyme, that used to grow above our house in Eze. Our summers were filled with it. Oh Christopher, where did you find it?'

Chris grinned. 'I thought we might fly down to the coast this afternoon. Italy's too hot in August, and the Riviera's really so busy nowadays. Provence? Too British. Florida? Too American. Thought instead we could try that big dune at Arcachon, with the long white drop towards the Atlantic, or sit in the shade of the pinewoods listening to the crickets and, in the background, the sea. Can you hear the sea?'

Now I *could* hear it: the soft *hissh* of water with a throatful of stones. Behind it, a burr of crickets; above me, the wind.

Hypnosis? Not quite; now I could see the Residents' Lounge tape recorder running; from the four big speakers came the sounds. Chris grinned again. 'Like it?'

I nodded, unable to speak.

'There's lavender, too,' said Hope dreamily. 'Blue lavender, that we used to sew into our pillows. And grass – cut grass – and figs ripening . . .'

More of those candles, I thought; but Hope's sense of smell is better than mine, and I could barely make them out. I could hear the sea, though, and the sound of the pines, and the *scree* of birds in a sky as hot and blue as any in those brochures.

Now Chris was on his knees in front of us. He took off Hope's shoes, then mine – Meadowbank slip-ons in sensible brown – and flung them (rules, rules!) across the room. Then, turning, he came back with a square basin, water slopping messily over the curved edges, and placed it at Hope's feet. 'I'm afraid the Atlantic's a little cold, even at this time of year,' he warned, and looking down I saw that the basin was filled with water and stones, the flat round pebbles you find on a beach. Hope's bare old feet plunged into the water, and her face lit with sudden joy.

'Oh!' Suddenly she sounded fifteen again, breathless, flushed.

Chris was grinning fit to split. 'Don't worry, Butch old love,' he told me, turning again. 'I haven't forgotten you.'

The second basin was filled with sand: soft, dry, powdery sand that tickled my toes and made small crunching noises in my insteps. Deliciously I dug my feet in – I can move them a little, though I haven't done any dancing in a long while – and thought back to when I was five, and Blackpool beach was twenty miles long, and the candyfloss was like summer clouds.

'After that lunch I don't expect you're hungry any more,' went on Chris, 'but I thought I'd try you on this, just in case.' And from some magical place at the back of the Residents' Lounge he brought out a tray. 'Not quite champagne and caviar, not on my budget, but I did my best.'

And so he had; there were canapés of olive and cream cheese and pimiento and thin-sliced salmon; there was chocolate cake and mango sorbet and strawberries and cream. There were iced whisky sours (*definitely* against the rules) and yellow lemonade; best of all there was no tuna, no egg and no pink fairy cake.

I hadn't thought I was at all hungry, but Hope and I finished the lot, to the final cracker. Then we paddled again, and then Chris opened the lounge piano that no one but he ever seems to play and we sang all our old favourites, like 'An Eighteen-Stone Champion' and 'You Know Last Night'; and then Chris and Hope did Edith Piaf with 'Non, Je Ne

Regrette Rien', and then we were very tired and somewhere along the line we both fell asleep, Hope and I, and
awoke to find the empty tray gone, and the water, sand and
pebbles gone, and the posters removed from the walls and
the danglers back on the chandelier.

Only the tape was still playing (he must have turned it
over while we slept). But although the candles were gone,
we could still smell them, grass and fig and lavender and
thyme, quite covering up that Meadowbank smell, and
when I popped back to my room I found the brochures
there, stacked tidily behind a row of books, with a note
from Chris lying on top.

Welcome back, it said.

I returned to the lounge just in time to hear the coach
pulling up into the driveway. Hope heard it too, and neatly
removed the tape from the machine before putting it into
the pocket of her dress. Neither of us spoke, though we
held hands and smiled to ourselves as we waited for our
friends to return: Polish John and Mrs McAllister and
Mr Bannerman and Mr Braun and poor Mrs Swathen, who
had, she said, lost her lace handkerchief on the beach, had
sand in her shoes and had surely caught heatstroke from
that horrid sun, it was a disgrace, no one knew how much
she suffered and if she had only known –

No one noticed, among that disorder, that we, too, had
sand in our shoes. No one saw us pick at our 'celebration
dinner' (rissoles) – unless it was Sad Harry, who never
talks much anyway – and no one seemed to care when we
went to bed early, Hope to smell the candles that Chris had

slipped into her bedside drawer, and I to read my brochures and dream of orange groves and strawberry daiquiris and plane rides and yachts. Next week we might try Greece, I think. Or the Bahamas; Australia; New York; Paris. If Tom can do it, so can we – besides, as Hope always says, travel broadens the mind.

IN PRAISE OF NARBONNE PLAGE

FI GLOVER

AT LEAST SOME THINGS IN life have a certainty to them. You always breathe in when you are trying to squeeze through a tight space in your car, somehow singing really loudly helps when you are dying for a pee, and as a woman you will never be able to emerge from the sea or a swimming pool without adjusting your swimsuit or bikini. Sometimes you try to effect this whilst still in the water – just a quick hoick to make sure that your nether regions are suitably covered, a sly glance to make certain that you aren't about to go a bit Janet Jackson. The exception is, of course, Ursula Andress, entering the world's conchiousness with that walk up the surf. Perfect, wasn't it? – but only because you *know* that in take one she had a sneaky tug around the buttock area and a fiddle with the halter neck before the director shouted an exasperated 'Cut!'

And so on the beach at Narbonne every woman emerging from the sea is tweaking and pulling and hoicking and checking. It's an age thing, too; it's possibly one of the firmest signs that you have left the innocence of youth behind you and entered the hormonally charged arena of adolescent life. For every woman it's a different age – for me I think it was about a precocious twelve. Before that I remained relatively carefree around water whilst wearing very little. But then came frosted pink lipstick, Anne French cleanser and that strong notion that there was going to be more to life than I had hitherto known. It was that glorious age of adolescence when you feel like a sneeze waiting to happen, and when the beach changes from being a place of certain, stodgy family fun into a strange land of self-consciousness and hormonal angst. Little do you realise then that you are going to have to wait another sixty years before you get to the equally carefree age when you let it all hang out again – in a more weathered, septuagenarian way. In between will be six decades of leg waxing, underwired support and numerous unsuccessful trials of self-tanning products.

On a sun-lounger in one of Narbonne's *plages privées*, I think that I can spot the French equivalent of myself at that turning age. She still has the podgy curves that I would now love to have, and the hair that curls up gently in the sun. Perhaps if she avoids the bleaching and dying then she can prevent hers turning into the straw that is now attached to my head, which, when dry, looks like someone has rubbed it with a balloon. *La petite française* is on the beach by herself, although the spare sun-lounger next to her looks as if it may be expecting a friend later in the day.

She's lying down facing the sea with her feet up on the raised headrest, iPod earphones in, foot gently tapping, just having a look around. I wonder what her summer has held? First kisses and hangovers? A sense of freedom or fear? She has a look on her face that's alternating between intense boredom and gentle curiosity. It's classic middle-distance staring look that teenagers of all nationalities can effect.

It's a look I like to think that I perfected during my adolescent years. I believe it was learned in chemistry lessons where in a couple of seconds I could switch from the boredom of reciting the periodic table to the curiosity of wondering why Mr Taylor wore such very tight white lab coats which gave him the look of an overweight cruise ship physician. It was not a particularly elevating part of my education. The only thing that seems to rouse *la petite française* out of the boredom that life obviously inspires in her is when the boys playing in the surf look her way – which is more often than their game of water ping-pong really calls for. They're playing just near enough to the beach to ensure an audience and create maximum disturbance. The four of them have that cocky pose that only tanned, fit fifteen-year-old boys can truly pull off. When they reach up for high shots you can see the winter white of their thighs – suggesting that like air-conditioning and rosé wine they are much more appealing in summer.

They have been hollering and whooping and splashing in the shallows for an hour at least, delighting in the fact that they have at least one nubile female onlooker. In fact, they have many more, as four ladies of a more certain age in the middle of the *plage privée* have also been watching their antics, with looks of envy and kind amusement. The boys are oblivious to their gazes. Their game gets even louder on the arrival of *une amie de la petite française*, who plonks herself down on the vacant sun-lounger. The iPod earphones are taken out and both girls turn their backs on the gang of four to chat as only teenage girls can. The ley line of unspoken teenage attraction from lounger to the shallows is temporarily broken and within minutes the boys give up their game and trudge back to their towels and bags on the other side of the *plage privée* fence – on the public beach.

Plage privées are found on most French beaches – and their name is somewhat misleading. All they consist of are parts of the beach cordoned off with windbreaks, where rows of neat sun-loungers and umbrellas are placed – waiting for you, the person who slightly fears the hoi polloi, the person who wants to feel a little more special in life, a little more privileged. It's kind of a Premium Economy beach experience – a little more legroom, a little more money and the *illusion* that you are being in some way exclusive.

On Narbonne Plage – with its miles and miles of open beach – there are several blue-and-white windbreaks that cordon off little private bits from huge expanses of public bits. And for just eight euros you can buy a sun-lounger for the day – with table and umbrella – and gaze out across exactly the same Mediterranean as those who haven't seen the need to pay for the privilege.

Narbonne isn't the kind of beach you will see mentioned in the Top Ten Beaches of the World in magazines like *Wallpaper* or *Traveller*. Their Top Tens always seem to exist entirely of stretches of white sand that are cocooned in privacy, with nothing but a wafting breeze to keep you and your £500 kaftan cool. And, of course, those kinds of beaches are beautiful in their exquisite, exclusive way – but oh! the boredom that must ensue from actually trying to spend a whole day on one of them. Even if you are with the one you love. The notion that by escaping everyone else you will be content is an odd one, propagated uniquely by travel pages with their constant message that 'getting away from it all' is the nirvana of life. Sitting staring out to sea with little or no company is the kind of thing that induces madness. Otherwise Guantanamo Bay would be a little more bearable. And have you ever stopped to wonder why all these beaches are so deserted if they are so wonderful? Where are all the other people who read *Wallpaper*'s Top Ten? Is it possible they arrived and only managed a couple of hours too?

I have tried the secluded beach experience only once – on a nature reserve in Mallorca, where we were dropped off in the morning with the promise that we would be picked up later on in the afternoon. Time ticked slowly by whilst the midday sun got higher and higher. We ate our picnic too soon and the beer started to get a little too warm as we jostled each other for some of the shade of the umbrella. We ended up playing alphabetical word games where we had to list world leaders alternately. It was almost as fun as Chemistry at school. Neither of us could get over the hurdle of 'Q', however, so we tried capital cities and realised that 'Q' was still a stumbling block, and had a row about whether Qatar had a city in it called simply Qatar. We abandoned that, but when we got to Chart Toppers of the Eighties, I would happily have started swimming to Menorca. Thankfully, another family turned up, zooming into view on their speedboat, and we could at least watch them. In fact, we ended up being extremely envious of the fact they had brought plastic inflatable dolphins, much larger sandwiches and had thought to have olive skin, which genetically enabled them to be on a beach in the midday sun. We should really have been hiding in the shade of a Constable haystack at midday – for good reason.

Perhaps the secluded beach thing is an age thing too. I presume that the success of Alex Garland's *The Beach* was because it tapped into that youthful desire to believe there is a world out there that no one else can get to – and that by reaching it you will find contentment along with a complete understanding of yourself. From my experience, there's little evidence in the huddles of gap-year students clutching Garland's epic that much is being enlarged except for their pupils of an evening.

Narbonne lies to the west of the long stretch of coastline that is the South of France. Go any further west and you will be in Spain. It's at the heart of plonk country with the bountiful vineyards of the Corbières and it's a place that seems very happy with itself. In fact, the current slogan for the city is 'J'aime ma ville – il y a de punch!' The actual city of Narbonne is slightly inland and has a stupendously magnificent cathedral, a central square where you can take the air and the wine of an evening, and a pretty canal running through it all. It's famous for having been the birthplace of the last of the troubadours, a Guiraut Riquier, who seems to have been somewhat of a melancholy soul and who left us all in peace in 1292. Because of its proximity to Spain, the whole area had pretty much non-stop trouble from the Middle Ages onwards. The Midi region was disputed by Visigoths and Saracens, by whoever was in charge of Spain and even by Paris itself. Now that things have calmed down, Narbonne is having a bit of a growth spurt in this new millennium – and there are plans to almost double the size of the city, plans that aren't universally popular. For the moment, though, it's a place where French families take their holidays, and on the beaches that stretch from Narbonne to Spain you can see why. This is a more grounded part of the French coast – it would be the sensible but pretty kitten-heeled shoe compared to the sophisticated but trashy Liz Hurley high-heeled sandal of the resorts further east. It has none of the boutique hotels of St Tropez, or the grand mansion living of Cap d'Antibes. You won't see George Michael taking in the promenade in Narbonne, or those coiffured French women taking their matching poodles and Chanel handbags for a walk in the late afternoon. Neighbouring Gruissan Plage made the area with its stilted houses a little famous in the film *Betty Blue*, but apart from that it's probably not somewhere you can automatically picture.

This is the last long weekend of the summer, late in August, when the French are savouring the remnants of *l'annuelle* before they head back to the cities for another year of crazy driving, eating good food and avoiding stereo-types like that one. It's been a long hot summer in the South of France, but the breeze is just about to change and bring in the cool air of autumn and the thunderclouds of September. Across the world it's also been the summer of Norah Jones – her tunes lurked around the pubs and bar-becues of London, they'd been hanging around the duty-free of the airport when we left, and now they are floating out over Narbonne Plage from the hut where the man run-ning the *plage privée* sits waiting for customers.

At eight in the morning there were only about a dozen of us on the beach – the sun-lounger man was waiting whilst an Algerian guy raked the sand for its litter of Marlborough Light fag butts and buried Coke cans. Once the sand had been suitably manicured he started chucking the sun-loungers down ready for another day of beach action. He looked as if he'd had a long season already. His face weary, his skin scorched by a summer out on the *plage*. He looked as if he needed some seriously shady months. His eyes looked straight through the nubile group of jog-gers bouncing across the firm sand. I imagine his gaze may have dwelt a little longer in the days of early May.

The beach has a life of its own that it completes every day. The early mornings are for the seriously fit: the run-ners and cyclists and rollerbladers, each zooming past on the concrete track above the beach, driven by some aerobic purpose and desire for what the personal trainers would call 'goal achievement'.

Mornings are for families, the little ones eager to widdle

in the sea and get their chubby bottoms in the sand, parents keen to leave the rented accommodation before the tearful *malhumeur* begins. A British family had been the first to arrive, weighed down with two toddlers and about twelve bags. My, my – the British don't travel light, do we? Is this some remnant from the empire, or our adventurous spirit in Africa? Stewart Gore Brown, an early settler in Rhodesia, penned in his diary that he loathed 'the kind of Englishman who travels with folding tables and enamel mugs'. It wasn't that he preferred the light option of a rug and a flask and a horse – he went for the full china dinner service and long wooden table on his trips out into the bush. Lucky, lucky servants. There seems to be something of this left in many modern-day British travellers. Perhaps some clever psychologist will turn this into a greater metaphor for our troubled minds – calling his book *Life's A Beach* and carefully deconstructing every meaning behind our unwillingness to leave the house without taking the house with us. This family of two parents and two toddlers would provide the perfect starting point for that theory. They'd brought string bags of toys, holdalls of food, rolls and rolls of towels, a big bag of books and suntan cream, and a spare umbrella for good measure. There were little bags hanging off the big bags and I suspect that inside those bags were a few more bags for good measure. Poor old Mum looked worried – hassled and troubled. When she ordered her nice new underwired bikini from the 'all sizes catered for' catalogue back home I bet she didn't imagine that her holiday would be this *detailed* all the time.

They settled only after everything had been unpacked, which was done whilst Dad looked on in a slightly helpless way that suggested he feared being put into a bag if he did something wrong. Mum had the pushchair-tan of an English summer – just arms and shoulders. Dad hadn't seen the sun for quite some time and was looking quite longingly at a copy of the *Daily Telegraph* poking out of the top of one of the bags. Meanwhile, four young Americans had arrived at the sun-loungers next door: two couples, all with glow-in-the-dark white trainers and matching teeth. They looked honed and preened and had the Manhattan accents that explained both those adjectives.

'Hiya!' screeched one of the girls in the direction of the sun-lounger man. It's possibly one of the worst greetings in the world, and a word that should only ever be said by Bruce Forsyth and followed by a cry of 'Lower!' from the audience. He sorted them out through a series of gestures and money changing hands. The Americans all looked a little exhausted by being away from their own territory, a slight look of fear behind the eyes at how this Europe thing works. It emerged that some of this may well have been caused by the fact that they are the kind of people who care more for their armpit hygiene than they do for the future of fossil fuels. They have all been suffering dreadfully from a lack of air-conditioning in their rooms at their hotel.

'Oh, but it's *so* not working – and I called the porter and he said they'd fix it, in like half an hour – and he *so* never showed up,' sulked one of the girls.

And so it went on. Please note my proper use of the word 'so' in that sentence.

Once they had calmed down, the most thorough application of suntan cream began, with much discussion about factor numbers. It is indeed a tricky thing going on the kind of holiday where you take most of your clothes off all the time. You don't really ever have to do that in Manhattan. In fact, I don't think you are allowed to take too much off in Central Park. And the sunshine poses such a problem. Tanning comes with the fear of ageing, and you don't really age in Manhattan – you just move to New Jersey and go out less. About four different bottles are needed to prevent this terrible thing from occurring: one for the legs, a special one for the nose, a big orange spray for the body and something approaching Farrow and Ball eggshell finish for the face. Of course, these sensible people are to be admired for their attention to cancer prevention, and if I lived in a country where it was a toss-up between being able to afford a house and having a mole removed then I would probably reapply more often. It got worse, though, as it also turned out that the girls have eaten carbohydrates on this visit. 'Cwa-ssants' to be precise. I imagine that penance will be extreme on their return to the land of skinny milk and antioxidant honey – it's quite possible that no bread or potatoes will pass their lips again until Thanksgiving. 2008.

By the time some kind of calm had settled at the *plage privée*, it was almost lunchtime. A couple of large French families arrived during the suntan application. Children of all ages spilling out from the shade of the umbrellas, possibly three generations, maybe four – it's hard to tell which of the still-svelte women is a mum. They are the lucky people to whom a beach is simply where you spend most of your summer. It comes with little ceremony and fuss, and lunch for each of them is simply a baguette sandwich, just the one – brought in a paper bag, no fuss, no plastic cutlery, no special containers of mini sausages and salads. No thermos of tea – just a munching old sandwich.

The British family have been ordered into the shade by Mum who has laid out all the above on one of the spare towels. It's a nagging affair of a meal – ending with some serious scrubbing with the Wet Wipes, which seems a little illogical. The Mediterranean is just ten feet away – why bring some soggy towels with their anti-bacterial promises with you? Your little ones have been widdling in the sea all day – as have about four hundred other people. It's unlikely that a moist towel will save them from a few runny moments.

It's mid-afternoon when everyone on the *plage privée* starts to notice the huge and growing bunch of Kiwis and Australians with the odd South African thrown in that has set up camp just outside the Premium Economy Beach Zone. What started out as a group of four of five, lazing quietly in the sunshine, has turned into a pack of about twenty – travelling their way round their late teens and the world with the deep tan, shaggy hair and friendship bracelets to prove it. Their body language suggests that many of them have had relationships with others of them.

Waves of laughter roll out from under their umbrellas every few minutes. They seem impossibly free. They look too big for Europe – they are a different, hardier species. The boys are musclier; they have flippers for feet, huge heads and beaked noses. The girls are so tanned even their armpits are brown. This summer's beach fashion for both the boys and the girls is the very low-slung surf shorts, which makes a British builder's bum seem like a modest option. Nearly all of them have a tattoo somewhere. One of the girls has some kind of Celtic symbol across her midriff, which you imagine might look like a map of the Norwegian fjords if she has a large family later in life.

With the sun at its highest, the rest of us have quietened down to a low murmur, flicking the occasional sand fly away and occasionally rousing in order to take a dizzying walk across the hot sand to the sea.

The Antipodeans are loud, though, and completely unaffected by the heat. They are variously involved in body boarding, a game of sand cricket, cracking open a few bottles of rosé wine and challenging each other to handstands in the shallows – a game I would be hesitant to play if the only refreshment available was rosé wine. But it's a wonderful sight – like a mini beach Olympics for the rest of us to gawp at without even having to sit up. They go on for hours without pausing for a rest. I'm pretty sure I'm not the only one on the beach who feels that I simply don't have the same chromosomes as they do. I can't even say that I used to be that energetic when I was their age – well, I could, but it would be a big fat lie.

The noise they're creating hasn't gone down well with everyone – I think I even heard some tutting from the other *plage privée* residents, especially when a newcomer arrived with a guitar . . .

By four o'clock the American contingent had become restless and headed off to look at the medieval city of Carcassone. 'It's meant to be so totally like awesome,' predicted one of them. Thankfully they wouldn't be as disappointed by that as they had been by their air-conditioning. The British family had toddled off to get another meal ready. There were tears involved in this process, and sadly Dad's copy of the *Telegraph* remained poking out of the bag, unread.

At six o'clock on the dot, the bored beach attendant asks the rest of us to start packing up, which seems like a sensible option to me and my reddened skin. It's that time of day when you know that the sunshine has baked your thoughts to their maximum optimism and to stay any longer would be foolish. As the sun loses its heat and height, the beach becomes the place for sauntering couples, and for illicit barbecues, spliff-rolling and the kind of drinking that leads you to imagine midnight swimming is a safe and fun thing to do.

By now the guitar is being put to good use in the Antipodean gathering – and all of the above seems pretty much a given. There'll be quite a haul for the Algerian man raking the beach tomorrow morning.

As I pack up to leave I can see the two young French girls trudging over the sand back to the town, looking longingly at the group. Maybe next year they'll be old enough and bold enough to join in the beach's late-night activity, but for now I suspect there is a nice family supper waiting for them at one of the well-kept villas back in punchy old Narbonne town.

But how wonderful to have all that beach action ahead of you, how reassuring to know that you don't have to search out some paradise idyll with matching hammocks in order to enjoy your sandy moments. How wonderful to be able to spend just one day in the company of all ages of man displaying all kinds of beach etiquette. How wonderful to have found Narbonne Plage.

FIRST SEA LORD

ADMIRAL SIR ALAN WEST GCB DSC ADC

In June 1972 my ship was slipping through the south-west approaches heading out into the Atlantic. It was the middle watch (0001–0400 hours) and the sea was glassy with no wind, but the beginnings of a very long swell gave us slight movement. Above was a vast canopy of stars. A trail of phosphorescence (caused by millions of plankton disturbed by the ship) left a magical green glow. However, it had been a different story the last time we crossed this particular patch of water.

HMS *Russell* was a Type 14 frigate; small by modern standards and reminiscent of the brave little escort ships that had ensured Britain's survival during the Second World War. She was built in the mid-1950s, designed for rapid production in shipyards all over the UK should the feared war against the Soviet Union happen. She had only one engine, one propeller shaft, two boilers and no stabilisers.

We had been returning from a visit to Bayonne, a French port in the south of the Bay of Biscay. The weather was foul. A string of autumnal gales had swept across the Atlantic and another deep depression was approaching.

The wind howled and the ship shuddered, creaked and groaned. Water was sluicing over the decks. It was hard for the ship's company to move around without being thrown into a heap on the deck or into a corner of some compartment. We had secured the ship by lashing furniture and wedging or stowing all movable equipment. The galley had produced 'potmess', an all-purpose stew, for those who weren't too seasick to eat.

Heading into the waves, we were rolling and pitching madly, but in the dog watches (1400–2000 hours) the ship turned in to the English Channel. Now the vast swell was astern and our motion became easier with the following sea. Because the weather had slowed us down, the Captain took the opportunity to increase speed to make our planned arrival at Portsmouth. The helmsman on the steering wheel found it tricky to keep a steady course because the large following sea made the ship's head veer wildly from side to side.

It was the last dog watch (1800–2000 hours) and most of those not on watch were lashed in their bunks. I was in the small wardroom with Andy, the First Lieutenant. We had wedged ourselves in the bench seats and were chatting about the time we had served in a minesweeper together. There was an unpleasant feel about the ship's movement and suddenly she broached. This happens when the following sea overtakes you and pushes her stern faster than the bow is travelling. The bow digs in and the ship rolls onto its side at right angles to the waves, or 'beam to sea'. The result can be devastating and has led to the loss of many ships.

As the ship began to roll I could see the whites of Andy's eyes, and I knew mine were registering the same concern. The roll seemed to last an eternity and we were thrown against the ship's side. There was a loud crashing as equipment broke free and catapulted across other spaces in the ship. The cords holding chairs and tables broke and they cascaded around us. All went black and then emergency lighting kicked in, bathing us in a ghostly glow. Alarms started ringing all over the ship. Still we rolled. There was suddenly the piercing howl of super-heated steam as the safety valves on the boilers lifted. Were we going to capsize completely? Would we survive?

The roll stopped and the ship recovered from what we later discovered was a 72-degree angle. The wave had broken over the funnel. We had lost all power and the ship was dead in the water, rolling like a pig, beam to sea. There was a smell of burning and people rushed to their duty stations. Mine was on the bridge. I rapidly confirmed our position and passed it to the main communications office in case we should need assistance. I then ensured that the officer of the watch had recorded everything in the ship's log.

It was a dark night and a large bulk carrier was bearing down on us, but our radios were unusable. Was he aware of our presence? When a ship cannot operate under its own power at night it must switch on two red lights to signal that it is no longer under command. With no power, we had to hoist two battery-driven lights on a rope lanyard. I grabbed two men and we went onto the flag-deck by the bridge, attached to lifelines. The ship still rolled violently and we were doused by heavy spray. It was impossible to talk against the screaming sound of steam escaping and the roar of the sea, but the lights were hoisted and a collision averted. Looking aft I saw stokers desperately working their way through pounding waves along the iron deck below to help in the boiler and engine rooms.

Thanks to good naval training, discipline and skill, power was restored and the ship got under way again. The smell of burning had been a fire in the galley where the chefs had started to make chips when we entered the Channel. They put out the blaze themselves and, still blackened with soot, continued to cook dinner for the ship's company. We berthed safely in Portsmouth, battered but not beaten by the sea.

I shuddered at the memory of this incident as HMS *Russell* cut smoothly through the glassy, phosphorescent sea. After handing over the watch to my relief at 0400, I stood a while on the bridge wing drinking a cup of traditional kye (a concoction made of condensed milk, hot water and chocolate shaved from a giant block). I marvelled at the sea's different moods and the fact that even the most experienced sailor must never underestimate its power.

THE BEACH BUTLER

RUTH RENDELL

The seaside resort in this story came out of my imagination. It's supposed to be somewhere on the coast of South America where the gulf between rich and poor is wide. I have never been there but I have been to Hawaii and it was on a beach there that I saw hotel servants combing the sands for lost jewellery and saw too the women who went swimming in a full panoply of diamonds. The story is a sad one because it shows how privation drives the poor to crime and that love is not always worth the price a woman may be asked to pay for it.

THE WOMAN WAS THIN AND stringy, burned dark brown, in a white bikini that was too brief. Her hair, which had stopped looking like hair long ago, was a pale dry fluff. She came out of the sea, out of the latest crashing breaker, waving her arms and crying, screaming of some kind of loss. Alison, in her solitary recliner, under her striped hood (hired at $6 a morning or $10 a whole day), watched her emerge, watched people crowd about her, heard complaints made in angry voices, but not what was said.

As always, the sky was a cloudless blue, the sea a deeper

colour, the Pacific but not peaceable. It only looked calm. Not far from the shore a great swell would bulge out of the sea, rise to a crest and crash on whoever happened to be there at the time, in a cascade of overwhelming, stunning, irresistible water, so that you fell over before you knew what was happening. Just such a wave had crashed on the woman in the white bikini. When she had struggled to her feet she had found herself somehow damaged or bereft.

Alone, knowing nobody, Alison could see no one to ask. She put her head back on the pillow, adjusted her sunglasses, returned to her book. She had read no more than a paragraph when she heard his gentle voice asking her if there was anything she required. Could he get her anything?

When first she heard his – well, what? His title? – when first she heard he was called the beach butler it had made her laugh, she could hardly believe it. She thought of telling people at home and watching their faces. The beach butler. It conjured up a picture of an elderly man with a paunch wearing a white dinner jacket with striped trousers and pointed patent shoes like Hercule Poirot. Agustin wasn't like that. He was young, handsome, he was wary and polite, and he wore shorts and white trainers. His T-shirts were always snow-white and immaculate, he must get through several a day. She wondered who washed them. A mother? A wife?

He stood there, smiling, holding the pad on which he wrote down orders. She couldn't really afford to order anything. She hadn't known the package excluded drinks and meals and extras like this recliner and hood. On the other hand, she could hardly keep pretending she never wanted a drink.

'A Diet Coke then,' she said.

'Something to eat, ma'am?'

It must be close on lunchtime. 'Maybe some crisps.' She corrected herself. 'I mean, chips.'

Agustin wrote something on his pad. He spoke fairly good English, but only, she suspected, when food was the subject. Still, she would try.

'What was wrong with the lady?'

'The lady?'

'The one who was screaming.'

'Ah. She lose her . . .' He resorted to miming, holding up his hands, making a ring with his fingers round his wrist. 'The ocean take her – these things.'

'Bracelet, do you mean? Rings?'

'All those. The ocean take. Bracelet, rings, these . . .' He put his hands to the lobes of his ears.

Alison shook her head, smiling. She had seen someone go into the sea wearing sunglasses and come out having lost them to the tide. But jewellery!

'One Diet Coke, one chips,' he said. 'Suite number, please?'

'Six-oh-seven – I mean, six-zero-seven.'

She signed the chit. He passed on to the couple sitting in chairs under a striped umbrella. It was all couples here, couples or families. When they decided to come, she and Liz, they hadn't expected that. They'd expected young unattached people. Then Liz had got appendicitis and had to cancel and Alison had come alone; she'd paid, she couldn't afford not to come, and she'd even been excited at the prospect. Mostly Americans, the travel agent had said, and she had imagined Tom Cruise lookalikes. American men were all tall and in the movies they were all handsome. On the long flight over she had speculated about meeting them. Well, about meeting one.

But there were no men. Or, rather, there were plenty of men of all ages, and they were tall enough and good-looking enough, but they were all married or with partners or girlfriends and most of them were fathers of families. Alison had never seen so many children all at once. The evenings were quiet, the place gradually becoming deserted, as all these parents disappeared into their suites – there were no rooms here, only suites – to be with their sleeping children. By ten the band stopped playing, for the children must be allowed to sleep, the restaurant staff brought the tables indoors, the bar closed.

She had walked down to the beach that first evening, expecting lights, people strolling, even a barbecue. It had been dark and silent, no one about but the beach butler, cleaning from the sand the day's litter, the drinks cans, the crisps bags and the cigarette butts.

He brought her Diet Coke and her crisps. He smiled at her, his teeth as white as his T-shirt. She had a sudden urge to engage him in conversation, to get him to sit in a chair beside her and talk to her, so as not to be alone. She thought of asking him if he had had his lunch, if he'd have a drink with her, but by the time the words were formulated he had passed on. He had gone up to the group where sat the woman who had screamed.

Alison had been taught by her mother and father and her swimming teacher at school that you must never go into sea or pool until two hours have elapsed after eating. But last week she had read in a magazine that this theory is old hat, you may go swimming as soon as you like after eating. Besides, a packet of crisps was hardly a meal. She was very hot, it was the hottest time of the day.

Looking at herself in one of the many mirrors in her suite, she had thought she looked as good in her black bikini as any woman there. Better than most. Certainly thinner, and she would get even thinner because she couldn't afford to eat much. It was just that so many on the beach were younger than she, even the ones with two or three children. Or they looked younger. When she thought in this way panic rushed upon her, a seizure of panic that gripped her like physical pain. And the words that came with it were 'old' and 'poor'. She walked down to the water's edge. Showing herself off, hoping they were watching her. Then she walked quickly into the clear warm water.

The incoming wave broke at her feet. By the time the next one had swollen, reared up and collapsed in a roar of spray, she was out beyond its range. There were sharks but they didn't come within a thousand yards of the beach and she wasn't afraid. She swam, floated on the water, swam again. A man and a woman, both wearing sunglasses, swam out together, embraced, began a passionate kissing while they trod water. Alison looked away and up towards the hotel, anywhere but at them.

In the travel brochure the hotel had looked very different, more golden than red, and the mountains behind it less stark. It hadn't looked like what it was, a brick-red building in a brick-red desert. The lawns around it weren't exactly artificial but they were composed of the kind of grass that never grew and so never had to be cut. Watering took place at night. No one knew where the water came from because there were no rivers or reservoirs and it never rained. Brilliantly coloured flowers, red, pink, purple, orange, hung from every balcony and the huge tubs were filled with hibiscus and bird of paradise. But outside the grounds the only thing that grew was cactus, some like swords and some like plates covered with prickles. And through the desert went the white road that came from the airport and must go on to somewhere else.

Alison let the swell carry her in, judged the pace of the waves, let one break ahead of her, then ran ahead through the shallows, just in time before the next one came. The couple who had been kissing had both lost their sunglasses. She saw them complaining and gesticulating to Agustin as if he were responsible for the strength of the sea.

The tide was going out. Four little boys and three girls began building a sandcastle where the sand was damp and firm. She didn't like them, they were a nuisance, the last thing she wanted was for them to talk to her or to like her, but they made her think that if she didn't hurry up she would never have children. It would be too late, it was getting later every minute. She dried herself and took the used towel to drop into the bin by the beach butler's pavilion. Agustin was handing out snorkelling equipment to the best-looking man on the beach and his beautiful girlfriend. Well, the best-looking man after Agustin.

He waved to her, said, 'Have a nice day, ma'am.'

The hours passed slowly. With Liz there it would have been very different, despite the lack of available men. When you have someone to talk to you can't think so much. Alison would have preferred not to keep thinking all the time but she couldn't help herself. She thought about being alone and about apparently being the only person in the hotel who was alone. She thought about what this holiday was costing, some of it already paid for, but not all.

When she had arrived they had asked for an imprint of her credit card and she had given it, she didn't know how to refuse. She imagined a picture of the pale blue and grey credit card filling a computer screen and every drink she had and slice of pizza she ate and every towel she used and recliner she sat in and video she watched depositing a red spot on its pastel surface until the whole card was filled up with scarlet. Until it burst or rang bells and the computer flashed 'no, no, no' across the screen.

She lay down on the enormous bed and slept. The air-conditioning kept the temperature at the level of an average January day in England and she had to cover herself up with the thick quilt they called a comforter. It wasn't much comfort but felt slippery and cold to the touch. Outside the sun blazed onto the balcony and flamed on the glass so that looking at the windows was impossible. Sleeping like this kept Alison from sleeping at night but there was nothing else to do. She woke in time to see the sunset. The sun seemed to sink into the sea or be swallowed up by it, like a red-hot iron plunged in water. She could almost hear it fizz. A little wind swayed the thin palm trees.

After dinner, pasta and salad and fruit salad and a glass of house wine, the cheapest things on the menu, after sitting by the pool with the coffee that was free – they endlessly refilled one's cup – she went down to the beach. She hardly knew why. Perhaps it was because at this time of the day the hotel became unbearable with everyone departing to their rooms, carrying exhausted children or hand in hand or arms round each other's waists, so surely off to make love it was indecent.

She made her way along the pale paths, under the palms, between the tubs of ghost-pale flowers, now drained of colour. Down the steps to the newly cleaned sand, the newly swept red rocks. Recliners and chairs were all stacked away, umbrellas furled, hoods folded up. It was warm and still, the air smelling of nothing, not even of salt. Down at the water's edge, in the pale moonlight, the beach butler was walking slowly along, pushing ahead of him something that looked from where she stood like a small vacuum cleaner.

She walked towards him. Not a vacuum cleaner, a metal detector.

'You're looking for the jewellery people lose,' she said.

He looked at her, smiled. 'We never find.' He put his hand into the pocket of his shorts. 'Find this only.'

Small change, most of it American, a handful of sandy nickels, dimes and quarters.

'Do you get to keep it?'

'This money? Of course. Who can say who has lost this money?'

'But jewellery, if you found that, would it be yours?'

He twitched off the detector. 'I finish now.' He seemed to consider, began to laugh. From that laughter she suddenly understood so much, she was amazed at her own intuitive powers. His laughter, the tone of it, the incredulous note in it, told her his whole life: his poverty, the wonder of having this job, the value to him of five dollars in small change, his greed, his fear, his continuing amazement at the attitudes of these rich people. A lot to read into a laugh but she knew she had got it right. And at the same time she was overcome by a need for him that included pity and empathy and desire. She forgot about having to be careful, forgot that credit card.

'Is there any drink in the pavilion?'

The laughter had stopped. His head a little one side, he was smiling at her. 'There is wine, yes. There is rum.'

'I'd like to buy you a drink. Can we do that?'

He nodded. She had supposed the pavilion was closed and he would have to unlock a door and roll up a shutter, but it was still open. It was open for the families who never came after six o'clock. He took two glasses down from a shelf.

'I don't want wine,' she said. 'I want a real drink.'

He poured tequila into their glasses and soda into hers. His he drank down at one gulp and poured himself a refill.

'Suite number, please,' he said.

It gave her a small unpleasant shock to be asked. 'Six-zero-seven,' she said, not daring to read what it cost, and signed the chit. He took it from her, touching her fingers with his fingers. She asked him where he lived.

'In the village. It is five minutes.'

'You have a car?'

He started laughing again. He came out of the pavilion carrying the tequila bottle. When he had pulled down the shutters and locked them and locked the door, he took her hand and said, 'Come.' She noticed he had stopped calling her ma'am. The hand that held hers went round her waist and pulled her closer to him. The path led up among the red rocks, under pine trees that looked black by night. Underfoot was pale dry sand. She had thought he would take her to the village but instead he pulled her down on to the sand in the deep shadows.

His kisses were perfunctory. He threw up her long skirt and pulled down her tights. It was all over in a few minutes. She put up her arms to hold him, expecting a real kiss now and perhaps a flattering word or two. He sat up and lit a cigarette. Although it was two years since she had smoked she would have liked one too, but she was afraid to ask him, he was so poor, he probably rationed his cigarettes.

'I go home now,' he said, and he stubbed out the

cigarette into the sand he had cleaned of other people's butts.

'Do you walk?'

He surprised her. 'I take the bus. In poor countries are always many buses.' He had learned that. She had a feeling he had said it many times before.

Why did she have to ask? She was half afraid of him now but his attraction for her was returning. 'Shall I see you again?'

'Of course. On the beach. Diet Coke and chips, right?' Again he began laughing. His sense of humour was not of a kind she had come across before. He turned to her and gave her a quick kiss on the cheek. 'Tomorrow night, sure. Here. Same time, same place.'

Not a very satisfactory encounter, she thought as she went back to the hotel. But it had been sex, the first for a long time, and he was handsome and sweet and funny. She was sure he would never do anything to hurt her and that night she slept better than she had since her arrival.

All mornings were the same here, all bright sunshine and mounting heat and cloudless sky. First she went to the pool. He shouldn't think she was running after him. But she had put on her new white swimming costume, the one that was no longer too tight, and after a while, with a towel tied round her sarong-fashion, she went down to the beach.

For a long time she didn't see him. The American girl and the Caribbean man were serving the food and drink.

Alison was so late getting there that all the recliners and hoods had gone. She was provided with a chair and an umbrella, inadequate protection against the sun. Then she saw him, leaning out of the pavilion to hand someone a towel. He waved to her and smiled. At once she was elated, and leaving her towel on the chair, she ran down the beach and plunged into the sea.

Because she wasn't being careful, because she had forgotten everything but him and the hope that he would come and sit with her and have a drink with her, she came out of the sea without thinking of the mountain of water that pursued her, without any awareness that it was behind her. The great wave broke, felled her and roared on, knocking out her breath, drenching her hair. She tried to get a purchase with her hands, to dig into the sand and pull herself up before the next breaker came. Her eyes and mouth and ears were full of salt water. She pushed her fingers into the wet slippery sand and encountered something she thought at first was a shell. Clutching it, whatever it was, she managed to crawl out of the sea while the wave broke behind her and came rippling in, a harmless trickle.

By now she knew that what she held was no shell. Without looking at it, she thrust it into the top of her swimming costume, between her breasts. She dried herself, dried her eyes that stung with salt, felt a raging thirst from the brine she had swallowed. No one had come to her aid, no one had walked down to the water's edge to ask if she was all right. Not even the beach butler. But he was here now beside her, smiling, carrying her Diet Coke and packet of crisps as if she had ordered them.

'Ocean smack you down? Too bad. I don't think you lose no jewels?'

She shook her head, nearly said, 'No, but I found some.' But now wasn't the time, not until she had had a good look. She drank her Diet Coke, took the crisps upstairs with her. In her bathroom, under the cold tap, she washed her find. The sight came back to her of Agustin encircling his wrist with his fingers when he told her of the white-bikini woman's loss. This was surely her bracelet or some other rich woman's bracelet.

It was a good two inches wide, gold set with broad bands of diamonds. They flashed blindingly when the sun struck them. Alison examined its underside, found the assay mark, the proof that the gold was 18 carat. The sea, the sand, the rocks, the salt, had damaged it not at all. It sparkled and gleamed as it must have done when first it lay on blue velvet in some Madison Avenue or Beverly Hills jeweller's shop.

She took a shower, washed her hair and blew it dry, put on a sundress. The bracelet lay on the coffee table in the living area of the suite, its diamonds blazing in the sun. She had better take it downstairs and hand it over the management. The white-bikini woman would be glad to have it back. No doubt, though, it was insured. Her husband would already have driven her to the city where the airport was (Ciudad something) and bought her another.

What was it worth? If those diamonds were real, an

enormous sum. And surely no jeweller would set any but real diamonds in 18-carat gold? Alison was afraid to leave it in her suite. A safe was inside one of the cupboards. But suppose she put the bracelet into the safe and couldn't open it again? She put it into her white shoulder bag. The time was only just after three. She looked at the list of available videos, then, feeling reckless, at the room-service menu. Having the bracelet – though of course she meant to hand it in – made her feel differently about that credit card. She picked up the phone, ordered a piña colada, a half bottle of wine, seafood and salad, a double burger and French fries, and a video of *Shine*.

Eating so much still left room for a big dinner four hours later. She went to the most expensive of the hotel's three restaurants, drank more wine, ate smoked salmon, lobster thermidor, raspberry pavlova. She wrote her suite number on the bill and signed it without even looking at the amount. Under the tablecloth she opened her bag and looked at the gold and diamond bracelet. Taking it to the management now would be very awkward. They might be aware that she hadn't been to the beach since not long after lunchtime, they might want to know what she had been doing with the bracelet in the meantime. She made a decision. She wouldn't take it to the management, she would take it to Agustin.

The moon was bigger and brighter this evening, waxing from a silver to a crescent. Not quite sober, for she had had a lot to drink, she walked down the winding path under the palms to the beach. This time he wasn't plying his metal detector but sitting on a pile of folded beach chairs, smoking a cigarette and staring at the sea. It was the first time she had seen the sea so calm, so flat and shining, without waves, without even the customary swell.

Agustin would know what to do. There might be a reward for the finder, almost sure to be. She would share it with him, she wouldn't mind that, so long as she had enough to pay for those extras. He turned round, smiled, extended one hand. She expected to be kissed but he didn't kiss her, only patted the seat beside him.

She opened her bag, said, 'Look.'

His face seemed to close up, grow tight, grow instantly older. 'Where you find this?'

'In the sea.'

'You tell?'

'You mean, have I told anyone? No, I haven't. I wanted to show it to you and ask your advice.'

'It is worth a lot. A lot. Look, this is gold. This is diamond. Worth maybe fifty thousand, hundred thousand dollar.'

'Oh, no, Agustin!'

'Oh, yes, yes.'

He began to laugh. He crowed with laughter. Then he took her in his arms, covered her face and neck with kisses. Things were quite different from the night before. In the shadows, under the pines, where the rocks were smooth and the sand soft, his love-making was slow and sweet. He held her close and kissed her gently, murmuring to her in his own language.

The sea made a soft lapping sound. A faint strain of music, the last of the evening, reached them from somewhere. He was telling her he loved her. I love you, I love you.

He spoke with the accents of California and she knew he had learnt it from films. I love you.

'Listen,' he said. 'Tomorrow we take the bus. We go to the city. . .' Ciudad Something was what he said but she didn't catch the name. 'We sell this jewel, I know where, and we are rich. We go to Mexico City, maybe Miami, maybe Rio. You like Rio?'

'I don't know. I've never been there.'

'Nor me. But we go. Kiss me. I love you.'

She kissed him. She put her clothes on, picked up her handbag. He watched her, said, 'What are you doing?' and when she began to walk down the beach, called after her, 'Where are you going?'

She stood at the water's edge. The sea was swelling into waves now, it hadn't stayed calm for long, its gleaming ruffled surface black and silver. She opened her bag, took out the bracelet and threw it as far as she could into the sea.

His yell was a thwarted child's. He plunged into the water. She turned and began to walk away up the beach towards the steps. When she was under the palm trees she turned to look back and saw him splashing wildly, on all fours scrabbling in the sand, seeking what could never be found. As she entered the hotel the thought came to her that she had never told him her name and he had never asked.

OUR SURFING ROOTS
Or why it ain't just a waste of time

ALEX DICK READ

THANKFULLY THEY HIT LAND, THOSE hardcore Marquesan canoe sailors who headed into the endless blue Pacific in a time before humans inhabited Hawaii. If their navigators hadn't skilfully pinpointed this tiny group of islands, the most remote landmass on earth, we probably wouldn't have surfing today.

Maybe we would. Coastal dwellers worldwide have always caught swells in their fishing boats when they landed on wave-fringed beaches. In Peru and West Africa certain cultures even worshipped waves, and sometimes rode them on special canoes and rafts. But none of them rode waves with as much skill and passion or made it a central, enduring part of their culture.

Those early Hawaiians did, which is what made their type of wave riding so different. They probably arrived on the islands armed with knowledge of canoe surfing, like their brothers and sisters throughout Polynesia. But some-where along the timeline they developed high-performance, twelve-foot wooden surfboards, designed for standing up on while riding big waves. How or why is not clear, but we do know that they really did surf, a lot, over a long period of time. Chiefs had a certain type of board, the *Olo*, which was the biggest, and made from wiliwili wood. They reserved certain spots, and the biggest waves, just for themselves. The lower classes, including women and children, rode the *Alaia* – a shorter board made from koa wood.

In this culture no one called surfing a waste of time. According to the earliest written records, which are consistent with the ancient legends of Hawaii, often, when the seas were going wild, daily life was put on hold and the people went surfing. At times like these there were fierce contests, heavy gambling and numerous rituals associated with the surf, performed to keep the hierarchy of gods happy and the universe in good order, or *pono*.

The first European explorers, who arrived more than a thousand years later, were quite simply amazed by surfing. Captain Cook had already seen people in Tahiti riding waves in canoes, but he'd never seen them ride these long thin boards, standing up. He devoted several pages to it in his diary.

Subsequent arrivals, Western churchfolk in particular, weren't so impressed. They did their best to wipe it out, which wasn't hard because the arrival of white men had set off an instant catastrophe in the islands anyway, as people died like flies from venereal diseases, influenza and other invisible genocidal weapons. The population plummeted in the years immediately after contact with the white men. By the time the missionaries started ordering people to wear clothes and build square houses, Hawaiians had already lost much of their culture anyway. So the ancient sport almost died out completely.

But the pulse never stopped. The heart of Hawaiian culture was still pumping, even in the late 1800s when a half-Irish, half-Hawaiian man named George Freeth made an old-style Olo board and began to ride it standing up in the mellow waves in front of Waikiki, the capital town of the islands. At the time, only a few Hawaiian families were still riding waves there, mostly on shorter Paipo body boards, as Hawaiians had since the days of King Kamehameha I, the great Hawaiian chief who took control of the whole island chain in the 1700s. The king, it is said, enjoyed surfing long into his sixties and was noted for riding enormous summer swells on the outer reefs of Waikiki.

As George Freeth and friends revived the Olo board, an increasing number of Hawaiians followed suit and surfing quickly became a major feature in Waikiki again. Full-time 'beach boys' did what their forefathers had done – hung out at the beach, surfed, fished and talked story amongst themselves. Only by now there were new spin-offs. Tourists. They loved watching these bronze watermen gliding with the waves, and as more and more arrived each year, more and more of them left with basic surfing lessons under their belt. The word was spreading to other lands. And Waikiki was emerging as something more than a busy port on a remote island. Its backdrop, Honolulu, was turning into an American city, and so popular was this seductive 'island lifestyle' that the authorities began using surfing, and the beach-boy image, to sell Hawaii as an exciting holiday spot for the super-rich of America.

One super-rich man, Henry Huntington, owned a little railway line back in southern California. He was so struck by the surfing he saw at Waikiki that he invited Freeth over to do a 'Hawaiian surfboard riding' display for the public. Freeth agreed, the people loved it, and Huntington left his name with the beach that some say still represents the heart of Californian surfing today. Much of what we call 'surf culture' these days originates, sometimes indirectly, from there. But it has never been a Californian thing, surfing. Hawaiians showed them how.

There were others in the islands who helped plant the seeds of the global surfing culture we inhabit today. Duke Kahanamoku, an Olympic swimmer, inventor of the front crawl and a Hawaiian respected around the world, decided he'd spread the knowledge of surfing to other nations whenever he possibly could. In the early days of the twentieth century, Duke covered a lot of miles – up the east and west coasts of the USA, and eventually across to Australia, putting on surfing displays wherever he went. And everywhere he went people were inspired by what they saw.

What Duke taught was a Hawaiian thing. He didn't just show people how to stand up on a piece of wood; he taught them to fashion the right shape and make the correct equipment for the waves they had. But it wasn't just practical. Duke also showed people a Hawaiian spirit of goodwill, which the islanders call *aloha*, and an attitude to life that is harmonised by the sea. As well as bringing the sport of his ancestors to these new countries, Duke was transmitting a 'vibe' from his own ancestral world.

Soon it went to Europe. The earliest known surfboard in this part of the world is a fine example of the Hawaiian spirit that comes in the package with surfing. It was a gift, sent in 1936 by members of the Waikiki Outrigger Canoe Club to an English dentist named Jimmy Dix, who lived in rural Somerset but holidayed in Cornwall each summer. He'd seen surfing in an encyclopaedia and written off to the club for information on how to build his own surfboard. One day some months later, a twelve-foot-long hollow wooden board made by Tom Blake arrived with the postman. There was a short note with it, which read: 'From the surfers of Hawaii, to the people of Great Britain.' With this one gesture of *aloha* many lives were to change.

French surf culture began soon afterwards, only this time through the prism of Hollywood when a film producer who'd surfed in Hawaii spotted similar, perfect waves in Biarritz. He shipped some boards over and made a few connections. Soon France too was tapped into Hawaiian energy, direct. And so it spread through Europe – in one country after another, people appeared on the beaches carrying long thin planks and playing the Polynesian way, in the most violent of seas.

Somewhere along the line the Americans had taken over Duke's role as chief messenger of the surfing gospel, spreading the good news of wave riding around the world through magazines, books, films. Perhaps the most effective of all evangelists were their servicemen, who surfed and left boards in Japan, Africa, the Caribbean, and dozens of other locations where people didn't yet know they could have fun in the ocean the way Hawaiians had done for centuries.

So too the Australians, who'd quickly become an expert water culture after the Duke's early visits and the growth of the lifeguard system. Aussies spread the art to the deepest corners of the East and reintroduced it, Hawaiian-style, to Pacific islands that historically had never passed the canoeing stage. They went all over the world as lifeguards and heavily influenced the surf cultures of Europe and South Africa. Others went deep, like Australian Peter Troy, a wandering 1960s surf monk who found sublime waves in deepest Indonesia and other parts of South-east Asia. He and other hermit-like disciples recognised nirvana when they saw it, but only because, a couple of generations back, Hawaiians had told them what it looked like.

Thus the sport of the original Hawaiian culture became a sport of the whole world – rich, poor and even landlocked countries cultivated their own surf cultures. In Brazil, surfers today are national heroes; in Israel there's a famous rabbi who surfs; in England you can do a university degree in Surf Science. In the Andaman Islands some local tribes saw surfing for the first time just a few years ago when a boatful of professional surfers explored the area; and Bulgaria's surf team travels for fourteen hours to surf knee-high windy radioactive lumps of water, Hawaiian-style.

So the sweet fruit that early Hawaiians grafted and

enjoyed for themselves over centuries produced the seeds of a new, global, surf culture. It is actually a sub-culture, which makes it less tangible, harder to understand for outsiders. Today, surfing is thick with diverse life forms and numerous mutations of the original *pono*-inspired play of ancient Hawaii. In fact, riding waves is probably the only thing we 'sub-cult' members have in common. That, and the way we do it, which in case anyone should ever forget, is wave riding, Hawaiian-style. Calls us bums, call us what you want, but hey, at least we're helping keep the universe in good order.

CONTEMPLATING ITHACA

MARY LOUDON

THEY SAY THERE ARE NO sharks around the Greek islands of Ithaca and Cephalonia but I know that's not true. I have seen a soap shark in Cephalonia, in Sami harbour, and it was approximately two and a half metres long and very heavy-looking. Of course, soap sharks are harmless to humans and more scared of us than we are of them. But I didn't want to meet one when I was in the water myself.

So it was partly about exploring my visceral fear of the deep, of the exotica lurking beneath (which translated itself into a fear of something identifiable, like sharks). And it was partly the idea of getting there under my own steam, a tiny dot of human being in that magnificent wilderness. But really it was the sheer beauty of the endeavour that made me decide to do it: to swim from the beach-garden of the villa in Fiscardo, Cephalonia, where we were staying, across the sea to the opposite island of Ithaca, hazy with distance, mysteriously indistinct.

I am obsessive about swimming. I swim nearly every day, a mile or so in my local pool, which is something I've done since my teens. If I can't swim because the pool's shut or there isn't time, I run instead, but I prefer to swim.

I've swum all my life. My aquatic background was a privileged one. I was lucky enough to grow up with a broad stream running through our garden, which my father and I dammed with large stones when I was little so that it was deep enough for children to swim in. There was also a good local swimming pool, plus two school pools that we were allowed to use, one of them outdoors. Such riches seem to me now almost an outrage.

On family holidays, I pestered constantly about being able to swim. It didn't matter what type of water, or where, or what temperature. I swam in the sea, in rivers, lakes, pools and freezing-cold mountain streams. I even threw myself, completely unbidden, into a couple of filthy canals. The first time, I was severely reprimanded; the second, I was violently sick. But like a dog that sees water and barks for a stick to be thrown into it, I cannot let it go unremarked upon. I cannot see it without experiencing instant longing.

Contemplating Ithaca with my three-month-old daughter in my arms, I considered my desire to slip into the waves beneath the bedroom balcony. That desire had a lot to do with physical and mental challenge, with being something insignificant in an overwhelming environment. It wasn't really so far off the beaten track from the delights and demands of new motherhood. It also had to do with adventure. Unlike the environments of the walker, runner, biker or skier, a distance-swimmer's terrain is mostly indoors, confined within an unremitting cycle of tumble turns. The

Ionian sea is a far cry from your average UK leisure-centre pool. The Greek islands themselves, like the Alps or the Bahamas, have a resolute identifying image: they are understood in a shorthand of golden sand and azure seas. A journey of my own across a stretch of water in such paradise, a journey probably uncharted by other swimmers, was a thrilling prospect.

We were on holiday in Cephalonia because we have friends who live there.

'You're crazy,' says Angelo, when I tell him what I want to do.

'Are you worried about the wind?' I ask.

The afternoon winds are notorious around Cephalonia. After midday the sea chops up as if someone were whisking it from above and it is suddenly easy to understand why the ancient Greeks believed in the wrath of the sea gods. Violent and unkempt, the afternoon sea lends itself naturally to a belief in creation's reward and punishment. Often the wind persists into the night, but by morning, just before sunrise, it drops and the water reassumes a look of blank innocence.

'Forget the wind,' says Angelo. 'There are terrible currents out there. It's a shipping channel. There are tankers. Really, this is a crazy thing. Dangerous. Don't go alone.'

Angelo and his wife Sophie have spent many years sailing. They live on a boat half the time. They have crossed the Atlantic, negotiated successfully with tyrannical storms. Angelo knows what he is talking about. But I have no intention of going alone.

'Come on, Angelo,' I say. 'Come with me in your dinghy. We'll go in the morning before it gets rough.'

'You want to swim to Ithaca? You're crazy,' says Angelo. 'My God, it's over two land miles.'

A couple of rounds at the leisure centre.

'You could go fishing,' I suggest.

'Okay,' says Angelo. 'So it's a fishing trip. Now you're talking.'

It's actually very easy to let go of land. The sensation of being released from it increases the further out to sea you swim, rather like watching countryside recede from the window of a climbing plane. As pebbles and sand gave way to an abundance of murky-brown weeds, and finally to nothing but the thick blue deep, I turned to wave at my husband and daughter on the villa balcony but could see them no longer. I put my face back into the water. There were no fish to look at this far out. Everything was too far below for me to see it. There was just the sunlight reflected and refracted back upwards in millions of silvery shards. I was wearing a snorkel and mask in order to swim most efficiently and so as not to choke on the waves. This meant that I had my head in the water almost the whole time, which was both good and bad for the imagination. Good was the glorious meditative state I found myself in, particularly in the middle of the swim, arms and legs in rhythm, sun dazzling upwards from beneath, so that at times I was almost able to kid myself that I was upside down, suspended. Bad was thinking soap shark, or octopus. The previous day, I had spied an octopus wound around the anchor chain of a small boat. It was so enormous that I persuaded myself for one insane moment of panic and ill logic that it was a drowned anaconda.

From time to time I raised my head to see where I was going. I was heading for a particular rock, a golden triangle rising from the water, and taking guesses as to its actual height. I had no sense whatever of the current that swept me nearly a diagonal mile from my chosen route. Moreover, it was only when I raised my head that I had any sensation of the tide or the effect of passing boats; and this was despite the fact that the vast tankers that pass equidistantly between each island create enough swell to make waves on the beaches one mile either side of them. I was surprised. Frankly, I had been expecting a bit of a fight in this watery outback. But conflict only happens where water meets obstacles and I was no obstacle. I was now a mere particle of the sea itself, subsumed. It was a wonderful feeling. Warm and silky, the water was so buoyant that progress was laughably easy. It was the most perfect swim of my life, body and spirit held in suspension, thoroughly alive yet completely disengaged.

I engaged pretty swiftly when I looked up to see a large tanker bearing down on me.

'Keep going,' called Angelo, 'it's half a mile from you.'

He was right, although for some time after it passed the waves were high enough that I couldn't see the dinghy at all. Briefly, I was alone, enclosed in barracking high waters.

My sense of security grew precarious, contingent entirely upon the restoration of the view.

The last half-mile was the oddest because the land, while growing closer, seemed always to be moving out of reach, assuming the impossibility of a rainbow. And then my triangular rock, which was not my rock at all but another like it, began to rise from the water. As the rock grew larger, and the seabed reappeared in opalescent gold and turquoise, ground rising from below and towering above, I felt the land closing its jaws. I reached the rock, slapped it hard and turned back towards the boat. Just as my exhilaration was assured my self-satisfaction was rightly subdued. For I realised as I surveyed the gorgeous aquatic desert behind me that I could never claim any kind of conquest over this environment, that even the mastery of my own body was dependent upon the shifting vicissitudes of the water. If I had achieved anything it was a glorious but accidental freedom: the liberation of belonging for an hour and twenty minutes in a world that does not belong to you.

KYLE

GERVASE PHINN

KYLE ARRIVED AT MISS DUNN'S classroom with the young head teacher two weeks into the new school term. He was small for his ten years, with a mane of dusty blonde hair tied back in a ponytail, a brown, healthy-looking face and eyes as bright and as blue as a summer sky. He was dressed in a bizarre mixture of clothes: baggy red T-shirt, denim jacket embroidered with birds and animals, grey cotton shorts (the sort you grow into), no socks and sturdy sandals.

'Ah, Miss Dunn,' the young head teacher said with his usual forced joviality and silly smile, 'there you are.'

Where else would I be, thought the teacher looking up from her desk without replying. Each morning, regular as the clock on her wall, she would be in her classroom marking the children's work and preparing for the day ahead. She had done it every day for all of the thirty-five years she had been in the teaching profession. She wasn't likely to change the habit of a lifetime.

The young head teacher, still holding the smile, directed the boy through the door with a gentle push.

'We have a new addition to our school,' he told Miss

Dunn, patting the child on the shoulder. 'This is Kyle and he will be joining your class.'

The teacher smiled at the strange little individual who stood before her. He stared around the room with wide inquisitive eyes. Surprisingly, for a child about to start a new school, he didn't look in the least nervous.

'Hello, Kyle,' she said pleasantly.

'Say hello to your new teacher, Kyle,' prompted the young head teacher before the boy could respond.

'Hello,' replied the boy cheerfully. 'How are you?'

'I'm very well, thank you,' replied the teacher, 'and how are you?'

'Well, I'm not too bad,' he replied, with what one might interpret as a cheeky smile. Miss Dunn wondered if he was being deliberately impertinent.

'I'll have a word with you at morning break, Miss Dunn, if I may,' said the young head teacher in more of a hushed voice. He gave her a knowing look – a look that said there were things about this child she needed to know. 'I'm now going to take young Kyle to my room and explain how we do things here at St Mary's. How we all behave ourselves, follow the rules, do our very best, how we all pull together and get along as one big happy family. We also have a school uniform here, Kyle, so—'

'My father's not into uniforms,' interrupted the boy.

'Well, I perhaps need to have a word with your father,' said the young head teacher with a slight edge to his voice. Then, turning to Miss Dunn, he told her, 'I'll bring him back at the start of the lesson.'

*

Miss Dunn did not return to the books she had been marking. She stared at the rain-soaked fields beyond the classroom window and sighed. Another child to add to an
already unwieldy class, she thought despondently. And
probably a little handful as well, by the sound and the look
of him.

At college, all those years ago, Miss Dunn's tutor, the
portly Dr Walsh, red-cheeked, barrel-bodied, fingers fat as
sausages, had told the would-be teachers the keys to educational success: high self-esteem, great expectations and,
of course, reading – the fundamental tool of learning. For
him, he had said, books 'are the architecture of a civilised
society, the window on the world'. Miss Dunn continued to
stare at the rain-soaked fields beyond the classroom window and she sighed again.

On hearing Dr Walsh's words all those years ago, Miss
Dunn had thought of her own parents: gentle, loving, ever
supportive. Hers had been a joyous childhood. She had
come from a home full of rich language and frequent
laughter, acceptable behaviour and family friends. A home
where there were positive attitudes to other people, and
books – lots and lots of books – and stories told and poems
recited. She had swum in an ocean of words: the Psalms of
David, the Parables of Jesus, 'The Flowers of St Francis',
the poetry of Blake and Byron, Lewis Carroll, Edward Lear,
Tolstoy's fables and fairy tales, *Gulliver's Travels*, *Treasure
Island*, *The Pilgrim's Progress*, stories of the Brothers
Grimm. Each night she would snuggle up to her father in
his great green leather chair and he would read to her in

his soft and captivating voice. He had died the previous
year, a sad, shivering old man, confused, struggling for
memories, entangled by words. At the end he had not
recognised her.

As she thought of the new boy, Miss Dunn wondered
what home he came from. He looked clean enough – not
the stained cardigan, grubby jeans and unwashed hair of
the neglected child, but who would send a child to school
looking like he did?

Miss Dunn had taught deprived children on leaving college; grubby little scraps from homes where there was precious little self-esteem and few expectations and, of course,
no books save perhaps for the big yellow ones under the
telephone. Theirs was a background of poverty, unemployment, family difficulties, absentee father, limited aspirations, few opportunities to better themselves and very often
verbal and physical abuse. She could tell by their sallow
complexions that their diet would be largely chips and
crisps and fast food and that they would be up most of the
night watching some unsuitable television programme.
She had seen it many times before. Those children hadn't
much of a chance but they were so appreciative, so grateful
to have someone take an interest in them, take the time to
listen to them. They had cried when she left.

The children who attended St Mary's had every chance
but there was precious little gratitude. They came from
affluent homes with parents who had high aspirations –
sometimes unrealistically high. They all lived in large
detached houses with their own bedrooms, they had

holidays abroad, their own computers and expensive bi-cycles. The new boy, this strange-coloured creature, just would not fit in. He was like some exotic bird caught in a flock of sparrows.

She could tell, of course, by the look on the young head teacher's face that the boy would probably spell trouble. No doubt the child's record from his previous school had been scrutinised, the catalogue of misbehaviour duly noted. Miss Dunn knew that the most well-adjusted and confident child would find it difficult starting a new school mid-term. It was never easy for the new pupil settling in, making friends, getting used to an unfamiliar environment, differ-ent routines and strange faces. For a child like this – so very different from his peers – it would be a nightmare. Oh yes, thought Miss Dunn to herself, it would prove very dif-ficult.

And, of course, he would have special needs. There was no question of that. His reading would be well below stan-dard, his writing weak and his number work poor. Miss Dunn thought of the disproportionate amount of time she would have to spend with the child to get him up to scratch. His inability to get on with the other children, his academic weakness and his lack of interest would manifest themselves in anti-social behaviour: angry confrontations, temper tantrums, truculence, rudeness, attention-seeking. She had seen it before.

Miss Dunn shook her head and looked down at the exer-cise book before her on the desk. The child's description she was marking, like all the rest she had read through that morning, was neat enough, the spellings were good and the punctuation sound, but it was tiresome in its predictability and banality. 'The sea was a lovely blue colour. Big waves rolled up the beach and covered the yellow sand. There were big cliffs and lots of rocks . . . ' She gave a great heaving sigh.

What had been the point, she thought, of spending all Sunday evening preparing a lesson that had clearly had so little effect? What had been the point of trying to fill the children with the same sense of awe and wonder as she felt whenever she saw the ocean? Better perhaps to have done what Mrs Waterhouse usually did with her class: give them a worksheet. 'It saves all that wretched preparation,' her colleague had told her casually. 'It occupies them, keeps them quiet and saves on the marking.'

Miss Dunn knew there was more to teaching than that. She had brought into school a selection of strangely shaped shells, fronds of dried seaweed, slivers of shiny jet, a variety of coloured pebbles, small jags of rock, fragments of smooth slate and polished amber, and arranged them on a table beside jars full of different-coloured sands. She had talked about her childhood and the walks with her father along the cliffs at Whitby. They would brave the cold wind and, hair stiff with salt, walk the clifftop path, looking down on the vast ocean beneath them, the forests of white crests, the grey waves curling and arching, the seaweed glittering wet. She had gathered the children around her and read a favourite poem: 'Sea Fever' by John Masefield.

I must go down to the sea again, to the lonely sea and
  the sky,
And all I ask is a tall ship and a star to steer her by,
And the wheel's kick and the wind's song and the
  white sail's shaking,
And a grey mist on the sea's face and the grey dawn
  breaking.

And all she got was: 'The sea was a lovely blue colour. Big
waves rolled up the beach and covered the yellow sand.
There were big cliffs and lots of rocks.'

Perhaps, thought Miss Dunn, it was time for her to go,
to leave teaching. She was nearing sixty and could retire
comfortably with her pension and lump sum. She might
join a night class, spend more time in the garden and take
up golf. Mrs Waterhouse, teacher of the eleven-year-olds,
who sat in the corner of the staffroom clacking away with
her knitting needles like Madame Defarge, spent most of
her time regaling anyone willing enough to listen with how
she was looking forward to finishing. 'I'll be glad to get out,'
was her recurrent announcement. 'If I had my chance over
again, click clack, I would never go in for teaching, click clack.
I've put my own children off, I can tell you that, click clack.
Standards have plummeted, click clack, children are so badly
behaved these days, click clack, parents are a pain in the
neck, click clack, and all this bloody paperwork, click clack!'

Miss Dunn had to admit that her colleague had a point.
It was tough going these days. Children were harder to
handle, parents were becoming increasingly demanding

and difficult, and the government buried teachers in a snowstorm of paper. Teaching was very different these days from when she started.

Miss Dunn had always considered herself to be a good teacher. She prepared her lessons meticulously, marked the books, mounted colourful displays, took children on school trips to the castle, the canal and the museum. She produced the nativity play each Christmas and coached the school choir. She knew that she would never win a 'Teacher of the Year' award but she was dedicated and hardworking and gave the children the best she could give. But her best was not good enough for the fat-faced school inspector, grinning like an overfed frog, who waddled into her classroom one morning clutching a clipboard like some gameshow host. He judged her lessons to be 'satisfactory'. Thirty-five years in the classroom and she is given the accolade of 'satisfactory'.

Then the young head teacher ('call me Gavin') arrived, bubbling with enthusiasm, bringing with him a bandwagon crammed full of every educational initiative and strategy that was doing the rounds and a new language full of jargon, psychobabble and gobbledegook. She had to smile. She could see the young head teacher describing the 'new addition' on the computer record: 'Kyle is a behaviourally challenged student from a multi-delinquent family with siblings high on the incarceration index.'

Soon after his arrival, the young head teacher had observed some lessons, 'in a bid to get to know all my staff'. At her first appraisal meeting he had informed her

('Please don't take this the wrong way, Miss Dunn, I'm just trying to be constructive') that she lacked a certain enthusiasm, the verve and vibrancy so necessary in the good teacher, that she did not 'sparkle' in the lessons he had observed. She told the young head teacher that she wasn't some sort of Christmas-tree fairy; she was a teacher with an unblemished record and over thirty years' experience. He had smiled in that patronising way of his and told her he wanted all the teachers at St Mary's to 'come aboard', 'think outside the box', become 'team players', 'get up to speed'. She had told *him* it was difficult to change at her time of life, 'for a leopard to change its spots', 'to put old wine in new bottles'. He informed her that they were 'not speaking the same language'. It was the first occasion she had agreed with him.

The bell rang shrilly and her reverie ended abruptly. A moment later the children burst through the door chattering excitedly.

'Quietly, quietly, children,' said Miss Dunn, clapping her hands. Kyle arrived by himself a moment later. He sauntered in with his hands behind his back. All eyes turned in his direction. There were whispers and smirks and a few giggles but he seemed oblivious and walked to the front of the classroom.

'That's right, come along in, Kyle,' said the teacher. 'You can sit down at the front.'

'Thanks,' he said, walking towards her with what she thought was something of a swagger.

The boy sat on the chair directly in front of her, rested his hands on the table and looked around him with wide inquisitive eyes.

'Now, children, look this way please,' instructed Miss Dunn in her teacher's voice. 'This is Kyle and he will be joining our class. I want you all to make him feel at home and help him to settle in.' She knew it was an idle request. None of these children would have anything to do with him. 'It must be rather frightening for someone to join a new school so I expect you all to be friendly and helpful.' The boy did not look at all frightened, she thought, catching sight of his serious face. Then she added, 'And if I hear of anyone being unkind in any way, then they will have me to answer to.'

When the children had settled down to their silent reading, Miss Dunn sat next to the boy and explained what they had been doing in the previous lesson. She noticed the fierce concentration on his face as he listened to her and the brightness of his large round eyes. There was a faint but not unpleasant smell of earth and leaves.

'We are writing a description of the sea,' she said softly, bending closer towards him. 'Here's a copy of the poem I've read to the class.' The boy scrutinised the sheet of paper like an accountant undertaking an audit. 'Don't worry if you find the poem a little difficult.'

'No, it's fine,' he said. 'No problem. I love the sea.'

'And you might like to look at some of the things on the table, the shells and pebbles, to give you some ideas.'

'Very good,' said the boy, fingering a shiny piece of jet. 'I've got quite a collection of shells at home and dried starfish and shiny pebbles. It's amazing what the sea throws up.'

'And try to think of the last time you were at the seaside and describe it,' Miss Dunn continued. 'Imagine you are on a beach—'

'Oh, I've been on quite a few beaches in my time,' the boy told her. 'Me and my father have camped on beaches. He says there's nothing like it, falling asleep under the stars with the sound of the sea in your ears and waking to the screeching of the gulls and the salty smell in the air. Sometimes on really dark nights, he lights a fire and reads stories.' The child suddenly became quite animated. 'He's got quite a lot of books, you know, my father. He calls himself a bibliomaniac. He gets them second-hand from the market or from charity shops. They never cost much, well, not the ones with the ripped pages and covers missing. *Hornblower*'s my favourite. *Moonfleet*, that's another. *Treasure Island*. I like listening to him read. I get away from things when I read.'

'And do you think you can manage to write a description for me?' asked the teacher.

'I'd enjoy that,' he said. 'The thing about the sea is that it changes. One minute calm and quiet, the next mountainous waves crashing on the cliffs. My father says it's like an untamed monster.'

'Good,' said the teacher, quite taken aback by the child's response.

Miss Dunn was taken aback again during the morning break. She had watched the boy in the lesson write slowly and with deliberation, his tongue sticking from the corner of his mouth. He occasionally gazed out of the classroom window, as if deep in thought; at other times he stared at the floor or closed his eyes as if in prayer. When the bell rang, the boy presented her with a neatly written and vivid description of crumbling cliffs, the cold grey endless sand and the foam flying free.

He couldn't have written this, she told herself. No child of ten could compose such a piece of writing. But she soon discovered that he had, and for the remainder of the week the boy continued to produce written work of such quality that Miss Dunn was spellbound.

'You have a real gift for writing, Kyle,' Miss Dunn told the boy one lunchtime. She found him in the school library poring over a book. 'I don't think I've come across anyone of your age who uses words with such richness and vitality.'

'Thank you,' he said smiling. 'I like words, Miss Dunn.'

'And how are you settling in?' asked the teacher.

The boy thought for a moment and a small smile came to his lips. 'I don't really settle in to any school. I've been to so many I think it best not to make friends and get used to things. My father doesn't like to stay too long in one place.'

'So you'll be moving on?' asked the teacher.

'I guess so,' he said. 'One of these fine days.'

'And how is the new boy faring?' the new head teacher

asked Miss Dunn the following week. It was morning break and he was pinning yet another government directive on the staffroom noticeboard.

'Very well,' she replied simply. She kept her exchanges with the new head teacher as brief as possible.

'He needs a good wash, from what I've seen of him,' Mrs Waterhouse observed from the corner of the staffroom, producing her knitting needles. 'And whatever is he wearing? He's like a walking jumble sale. I wasn't aware the school rule on uniform had been relaxed.'

'I have to disagree with you there, Doris,' said Miss Dunn. 'He's a very clean boy and, what's more, he's highly intelligent and very well behaved.'

'The school rule on uniform has most certainly not been relaxed,' said the new head teacher, clearly stung by his colleague's comment. 'I have written to his father on two occasions but received no reply.'

'His father's not into uniforms,' Miss Dunn told him mischievously, echoing the boy's own response.

'Well, I am,' said the new head teacher, drawing pin poised. 'I predicted that he would be something of a problem.'

'He isn't,' replied Miss Dunn.

'I would never have guessed from the look of him, click clack,' said Mrs Waterhouse. 'He looks a very odd child, quite bizarre, I should say.'

'Appearances can be deceptive, Doris,' said Miss Dunn.

'He doesn't seem to mix,' said the new head teacher. 'I was monitoring him from my window at afternoon break yesterday. He was sitting on the wall by himself with a book. Perhaps I ought to get the educational psychologist to have a word with him.'

Perhaps you ought to leave him alone, Miss Dunn thought to herself. 'Some people do enjoy their own company,' she told him. 'And some people do like to read. He seems happy enough.'

'Is he bullied?' asked the new head teacher. 'Loners like him and children who are perceived to be different tend to get bullied.'

'No, he isn't bullied,' said Miss Dunn.

'One can't be too sure,' said the new head teacher.

'I am,' said Miss Dunn.

'What's his background, click clack,' asked Mrs Waterhouse. 'Looks like a little gypsy to me.'

'We don't say "gypsy" any more, Mrs Waterhouse,' the new head teacher told her pompously. 'The term we now use is "traveller".'

'Well, I would watch your purse, Dorothy, if I were you, click, clack,' Mrs Waterhouse said.

'I would be grateful, Miss Dunn,' said the new head teacher, 'if you speak to him about the uniform. We can't have him coming to school dressed like that, and I think you also need to have a word about the length of his hair and those sandals. Quite inappropriate for St Mary's.'

'I thought this was a church school,' said Miss Dunn.

'It is a church school,' replied the new head teacher.

'Well, long hair and sandals were good enough for Jesus,' she told him before leaving the staffroom.

*

The following Saturday afternoon as she was making her way through the small arcade in the centre of the town, Miss Dunn came upon Kyle. He was holding out the lid of a biscuit tin as shoppers passed by, begging for change, but his eyes were set firmly on a man trying to get a tune out of a fiddle and dancing, dancing very badly. He was a tall striking-looking individual with long blonde hair tied back in a ponytail and bright but shabby clothes. His boots clattered as he brought them down heavily on the pavement. Miss Dunn watched, fascinated. When the man stopped and scooped up the few coppers in the tin lid, she approached.

'Hello, Kyle,' she said.

If he was embarrassed, he didn't show it. 'Hello, Miss,' he replied.

The tall individual swivelled around.

'This is my teacher.'

'Hello,' said Miss Dunn pleasantly.

'How do you do,' replied the man, and stared at her with eyes as bright and as blue as a summer sky.

'My father's a dancer and a fiddle player,' said the boy proudly. 'He's a street entertainer.'

'So I see.'

'I hope Kyle is not giving you any trouble,' said the boy's father.

'Not at all,' replied Miss Dunn. 'In fact, it's been a pleasure to teach him.'

'Good,' said the man, smiling and putting a hand on his son's shoulder. 'He's a good boy.'

'I would like to talk to you about Kyle,' said Miss Dunn, as the man began to put the old violin in a battered case.

'If it's about the uniform, you're wasting your time. I dislike any kind of uniform. We are all different, Miss Dunn.'

'Actually, it's not about the uniform,' said the teacher. 'I would like to discuss Kyle's work. Perhaps you might like to call into school some time.'

'I don't like schools,' said the man. 'Never have. Never will. They teach children things not worth knowing. They try and change you. We don't need schools. The only reason my son is at school is they'd have me up in court again or try and put him in care.'

'Nevertheless—' Miss Dunn began.

'Look, Miss . . . '

'Dunn.'

'Look, Miss Dunn,' said the man, moving closer to her. 'Kyle and me, we get on well without school, we do all right. We don't want people trying to change us.'

'I like Miss Dunn, father,' said Kyle. 'She's the best teacher I've had. She doesn't try to change you.'

'Well, I'm grateful for that,' said the boy's father, 'but it won't be long now before we're moving on.'

'You're leaving?' asked the teacher.

'We never stay in one place for long,' said the man. 'We like to travel, see the world.'

'That is a pity,' said Miss Dunn. 'I'll be sorry to see Kyle go.'

'Thank goodness for small mercies,' said Mrs Waterhouse in the staffroom the following week. She was rootling in her shopping bag for her knitting.

'Did you say something?' asked Miss Dunn.

'That gyspsy child who was in your class. He's gone. Well, that's what our esteemed leader told me this morning. I should think you're as relieved as he is.'

'Relieved?' repeated Miss Dunn. 'And why should I be relieved?'

'He was a little urchin, quite out of place at a school like this. He stood out like the proverbial sore thumb, didn't mix, no uniform. Of course, they never stay long, these gypsy types, and they're a damn nuisance when they are here. Well, it's one less for you to worry about and I am certainly not shedding any tears that he won't be in my class next term. I can't have put my knitting in. That's a devil. I wanted to finish that jumper this week.'

'He was a nice little boy,' said Miss Dunn to herself.

'What?' asked her colleague.

'Kyle, he was a nice little boy and very clever too,' said Miss Dunn. She took the sepia postcard of the harbour at Whitby, showing the gaunt abbey high on the cliff, the estuary crammed with boats, and beyond the great sweep of sand and the vast ocean. It was from the boy.

'I shall miss him,' murmured Miss Dunn.

'Did you say something, Dorothy?' asked her colleague, who, having found her knitting, was adjusting her needles.

'I said I shall miss him,' said Miss Dunn loudly.

'You do say the strangest things, Dorothy Dunn,' said her colleague, clacking her needles with a vengeance.

THE SAILING LIFE OF
RANDALL WILLEY

JAMES LANDALE

'HOLD TIGHT.' RANDALL WILLEY'S BOOMING voice cut through wind and rain to the crew cowering below. 'This one's going to be big.' The world-renowned sailor stood alone at the wheel, his eyes locked on the wave about to break over the stern of the yacht. A deluge of green water poured into the cockpit, submerging Randall so completely that he disappeared from sight. But somehow, miraculously, he emerged from the flood, shaking water but not the smile from his face. Shakespeare was wrong, he thought. It's not love that looks on tempests and is not shaken. It's men, men who are prepared to take whatever the sea throws at them. 'Are we going to make it?' a face cried from the companionway. A pale, fear-ridden face, drained of all artifice. Randall looked down. He pitied the crew, most of whom were lashed to their bunks, numbed by the ceaseless ferocity of the storm. 'Of course we shall,' he shouted to the hooded figure. 'We're going to be fine.' Another wave slammed into the boat. Calm, absorbed in his task, Randall used all his experience to control the wheel, skilfully keeping the sea at his stern as he steered the yacht obliquely down each wave to slow its descent. All the while, his brilliant mind navigated furiously, mentally computing their position from charts stored away in his photographic memory. Suddenly the boom swung loose on the main sheet track and started thumping insistently to windward.

'Randall!' Mrs Willey inclined her head only a few inches when she spoke to her husband so as not to waste too much of the sunlight being reflected onto her neck from the mirror beneath her chest. 'The washing machine's playing up again.' She was sitting, as she always did, semi-naked athwart the sun-lounger on the foredeck. Her legs were spread inappropriately wide so they could catch as much sun as possible. The mirror lay just above her crotch, propped up on a pile of old glossy magazines.

For a second or two, Randall looked at her in blinking astonishment, the storm fading quickly into the recesses of his mind. In its place came the unexpected thought that his wife, thus exhibited, resembled a duck cooking gently in the window of a Chinese restaurant, crouched in sweaty rigor mortis, growing ever more shrivelled and brown as the day wore on. He struggled with the image for a moment, his incomprehension total, before he shook his head clear and turned to the loud throbbing coming from below. He did not care for the washing machine. Mrs Willey had insisted on it as a condition of her presence on the boat. But somehow it did not feel quite right. It was not just that it took up so much space. A washing machine, of course, did not just mean a washing machine. It meant installing a water-maker too. Mrs Willey had made it quite clear that she wasn't going to wash her smalls in seawater, thank you very much. Both machines consumed so much electricity that Randall had had to buy a bigger generator. This, in turn, left the boat even more cramped, and even heavier in the water, points that held no sway with Mrs Willey, whose nautical ambitions were limited to sunbathing on a deck that was attached firmly to a marina pontoon. To Mrs Willey, a boat was simply a platform for her perpetual battle with pallor.

But, Randall's disapproval of the washing machine went further than the merely practical. He had a nagging suspicion that somehow it was unseamanlike. He did not think Sir Robin Knox-Johnston had washing machines on his boats. Sir Robin was Randall's secret hero, an icon amongst yachtsmen he worshipped in private away from the self-consciousness of the sailing-club bar. Randall envied what he called 'the cut of Sir Robin's jib' – Randall was a dedicated user of nautical cliché; it made him, if nothing else, feel more of a seaman – and he admired Sir Robin's weather-beaten, bearded appearance, the way he looked as if he had just stepped off a boat, a spare length of line always to hand, just in case there was a sail that needed furling or a spar made fast. No, Randall sighed to himself: Sir Robin Knox-Johnston definitely doesn't have washing machines on his boats.

'Randall, what are you waiting for?' Mrs Willey was becoming insistent. 'How many times do I have to tell you? You know my head's been killing me all morning. That racket is not making it any better.' Randall stepped below and gave the washing machine a clumsy kick and the banging gave way to a less violent rat-tat-tat-tat. He climbed slowly back up the companionway and resumed his seat in the cockpit so he could continue his study of the other boats. The marina was packed, heaving with neglected wealth, floating fridges whose lines were rarely slipped. Most of the yachts, like Randall's, were white and French, flat-bottomed cruisers built for charter and the unknowing rich. Most, however, were bigger than Randall's boat, a modest 28-foot sloop that aspired to cross oceans but rarely left port. He had almost bought the 32-footer in the catalogue but had inevitably gone for the cheaper option, deluding himself that four feet would not make much difference. He knew now how wrong he had been, but it was too late; his boat was poky and that was that. He contented himself instead by looking down, literally and figuratively, on those craft smaller than his: the day-boats, the luggers, the dinghies. But his eyes were drawn inexorably to the glorious, magnificent J-Class super-yacht, bobbing in the breeze like the thoroughbred that she was, tied up to her personal pontoon at the far end of the marina, her halyards tapping briskly against the mast.

Randall stared up at the mountain of canvas and spars soaring above him into the sky. Each sail was sheeted tidily home, each driving the boat on. Conrad, he remembered, talked of the 'preposterous tallness' of sailing ships. How true that was! In his hands, the wheel felt sure and firm, just a fraction of weather helm as he steered all ninety foot of super-yacht hard on the wind. 'Make fast that line!' he roared at a crewman, narrowing his eyes as he squinted beyond the bow. 'Aye, aye, Mr Willey.' Randall had enough to think about already without having to worry about some damn-fool hand not doing his job. 'Gusting, gusting,' a voice cried from the rail and the yacht heeled hard over. Others might have let off some sail, powering the yacht down, easing the pressure on the shrouds and stays. But not so Randall Willey. The billionaire industrialist and holder of the America's Cup was not known for his caution. He had a mark to make and a race to win, and a few gusts were not going to get in his way. The leeward rail dipped beneath the water, sending puffs of spray aft. But none of the crew were worried. For at their helm they had Randall Willey, possibly the best helmsman in the world, and if he was confident they would reach the buoy on this tack, then that was good enough for them. Randall pulled his cap closer over his eyes, reading the wind like a pilot, riding the boat like a jockey. A wave bounced off the bow, sending an arc of cool water tumbling into the stern.

'For God's sake Randall, can't you even hold your drink these days?' He looked down at his trousers where a large, dark patch was spreading moistly across his lap. He had spilt his gin. 'On your special trousers, too.' Mrs Willey was particularly proud of his trousers. They were red canvas, of a type she had seen worn by other sailors. She cared little for Randall's hobby but took the view that if her husband was going to do something, at the very least he should look the part. So she had bought him a blue blazer with brash gold buttons from Austin Reed, and a white peaked cap from an advert she had seen in the back of one of the magazines they had at the hairdresser's. And the red trousers. Randall did not like the trousers and was not unhappy to have spilt gin over them. The thing was, Mrs Willey had not quite got the colour right. The trousers worn by other sailors, as far as he could see, were of a lighter, more pastel red, as if faded by sun and salt. His trousers were of a brighter, bolder rouge, and tighter than perhaps they ought to have been. They were, to Randall's mind, trousers of the sort more traditionally worn by children's television presenters of ambiguous sexuality than by hardened sea dogs. So it was with some relief that he went below to change. Above him, his wife tottered over the deck, her stilettos scoring yet more marks in the already pocked teak. Randall winced but, as always, said nothing.

'I'm going shopping,' Mrs Willey announced down the companionway. 'If you haven't already forgotten, which of course you have, so I'm reminding you anyway, next door are coming for tea and we need some more sparkling rosé.'

Randall sighed. He had forgotten to go to the off-licence that morning and she had not let him forget it. 'They'll be quite happy with some Chardonnay,' he said in token protest.

'We've been through all that,' Mrs Willey replied sharply. 'The book was quite clear: "sparkling rosé is eminently suitable to serve on board a yacht". I remember it distinctly.' With that, she stood up, wrapped her corpulent midriff in the sarong she had been persuaded had come from Thailand, and picked up her handbag. 'Now. When I come back, I want everything tidied up downstairs.'

'Below,' Randall muttered under his breath; 'it's not downstairs, it's below.'

'I want everything tidied up downstairs,' she repeated, ignoring him. She paused, looked at her husband with a now familiar mixture of loathing and contempt. 'So, can I trust you enough to leave you alone for twenty minutes?'

Randall Willey stood at what was left of his mast, alone with the sea, his battered yacht carving a gentle path through the water at a steady four knots. He looked up at the jury rig, as he had every day, every hour, every minute of the last three months to check the sail, such as it was. Randall smiled a toothy smile through the tufts of his beard and thought: She's got me this far, she'll get me home now. His gaze shifted to the sun, high in the sky. Almost noon, he thought, and went below for his sextant. He took a few sights, looked at his watch, and did some astonishing mental arithmetic. 'Not far now,' he concluded. 'Not far now.'

The world-famous solo sailor had set out from France five months earlier to race alone around the world. But two months in, deep in the Southern Ocean, a wave to end all waves had turned his boat over and woven his rigging into a knot of steel spaghetti. His food was ruined, his water tanks breached and his electricity generator broken. But he had not given up. Oh, no, not Randall Willey. Not the man who had taught Ellen MacArthur everything she knew. He constructed a jury rig as best he could and sewed himself a new sail. He survived on raw fish and kelp, washed down by rainwater. He navigated as he had done as a child, by the stars and the sun, a true sailor shorn of modern fripperies and technology, relying on the essentials that had seen mariners safely home for thousands of years. And now, after all those days at sea, he was almost home. Already, despite everything, he was not looking forward to the attention his heroic return would receive. Perhaps he should simply carry on sailing, like the great Bernard Moitessier, and just pass the finish line and Britain by. But his reverie was broken by a faint buzzing on the horizon, a sound that became steadily louder as he made out the helicopter flying low over the waves. And so it begins, he thought. The aircraft swept past him, banked steeply and returned to take up a position just off the port bow, the sound of its engines ever more plangent, the vwoop, vwoop of the blades drumming into his head . . .

Randall sat up with a start. Someone was thumping on the side of the boat. He popped his head out of the hatch and saw his wife standing on the pontoon, bags of shopping at her feet. She was furious; he could tell from the way the fake tan on her face had turned a deeper orange and the sunburn on her cleavage glowed. The world's most famous solo sailor said nothing, but helped his wife up the steps and collected the shopping bags. He watched as she squeezed sideways through the bulkhead door to the cabin, carefully protecting her new perm from any navigational hazards on the ceiling. She was talking but, to Randall, her voice had that faraway, disjointed feel, like the crackling chatter of a VHF radio that everyone ignores until the fearful trigger-word 'Mayday' startles and pricks the ears. Yet the word never came. Randall unpacked the shopping and stood in the galley, desultorily washing up the cups in the sink, and soon was far, far away.

Randall's boat was about to sink and sink fast. He knew it instinctively, he could feel it in his seaman's bones. The craft was waterlogged, waves lapping over the gunwales as the ocean poured in below through the ruptured hull. There was no alternative. Without hesitation, Randall took out a knife and cut the line to the life raft. Had he not acted so swiftly the sinking yacht would have dragged the raft down with it, sucking his six crew to their breathless deaths. This was their only chance. Too bad he couldn't join them. 'What have you done?' they cried as their raft floated rapidly away. 'Don't worry,' the skipper shouted. 'It's for the best.' And they watched as Randall Willey stood at the mast, proud, upright, the water at his feet, a final cigarette playing about his lips, as he did what captains did and went down with his ship.

CHRISTMAS AT SEA
Suhaili, 25 December 1968

SIR ROBIN KNOX-JOHNSTON

Extract from the diary written on Christmas Eve and Christmas Day 1968 by Robin Knox-Johnston aboard the yacht Suhaili, some 2,000 miles from Cape Horn in the Roaring Forties of the Southern Ocean, while making the first solo non-stop circumnavigation of the world. The voyage started from Falmouth, UK, on 14 June 1968, and was completed 312 days later on 22 April 1969.

CHRISTMAS IS VERY MUCH A family festival at home or on board ship, and indeed my last eleven Christmases had been spent on British India Ships. The thought of being by myself at Christmas rather ruffled me. For almost the first time since I left Falmouth I felt that I was missing out on something, and that perhaps it was rather stupid to spend a whole year of one's life stuck out on one's own away from all the comforts and attractions that home offers. By now, Dad and my brothers would have brought in logs from the old trees in the garden, and the family would be clustered round a roaring fire in the drawing room, and thinking of going to midnight service at the village church in Downe. I recalled winter evenings at home when we played bridge. The memory of Mother as my partner humming 'Hearts And Flowers' and Diana asking Dad if she could go 'Crash' or 'Slosh' had me roaring with laughter. The warmth and fellowship of those scenes seemed to be in such contrast to my present circumstances that I brought out a bottle of whisky, feeling that if I couldn't have the fire, I could at least give myself an inner glow.

Two glasses later I clambered out on deck and perched myself on the cabin top to hold a carol service. I sang happily away for over an hour, roaring out my favourite carols, and where I had forgotten the words, singing those I did know over again. By the time I had exhausted my repertoire and had a few encores I was feeling quite merry. Christmas, I reflected as I turned in, had got off to a good start after all.

The first words in my diary for December 25th are 'Awoke feeling very thick headed'. Despite this, at 9 a.m. I drank to those at home, where the time was 6 p.m., and then began preparing a currant duff. I made an effort over Christmas lunch. I fried a tin of stewed steak and had potatoes and peas, cooked separately for a change, and to go with them I opened the bottle of wine that my brother Mike had given me and which I had been saving for this occasion. I rather overestimated on the quantity, though, and it filled me up, so the duff had to wait until the evening before I could tackle it, by which time it had gone soggy.

At 3 p.m. I drank a loyal toast, wishing that I had been up early enough to hear the Queen's speech at 6 a.m. my time. Somehow, gathering together to listen to this speech adds to the charm of Christmas. One becomes aware of people all over the world held by the same interest listening as well, and it makes the world seem a lot smaller. I wish that it was!

In the evening I tried without success to call up New Zealand and Chilean radio stations; then I listened in to some American commercial stations that were coming through rather well. There must have been unusual radio conditions as I was able to pick up local stations from Illinois, Texas and California, and it was on the last that I heard a recording from the 1968 manned American moon shot. I had not heard before of *Apollo 8* and her crew, the first men actually to go round the moon, and it gave me food for thought. There they were, three men risking their lives to advance our knowledge, to expand the frontiers that have so far held us to this planet. The contrast between their magnificent effort and my own trip was appalling. I was doing absolutely nothing to advance scientific knowledge; I would not know how to. Nothing could be learned of human endurance from my experiences that could not be learned more quickly and accurately from tests under controlled conditions. True, once Chichester and Rose had shown that this trip was possible, I could not accept that anyone but a Briton should be the first to do it, and I wanted to be that Briton. But nevertheless to my mind there was an element of selfishness in it. My mother, when asked for her opinion of the voyage before I sailed, had replied that she considered it 'totally irresponsible', and on Christmas Day I began to think she was right. I was sailing round the world simply because I bloody well wanted to – and, I realised, I was thoroughly enjoying myself.

A WORLD IN PIECES

JULIE MYERSON

So we're on the road, a long time ago, in this long shiny car of his with the roof down and it's the thickest, hottest part of the afternoon – everyone else is sleeping in the shuttered cool right now – but not us, we're driving in this hard, mad way through the baking dust and I can't help noticing that he's taking the corners viciously, like he wants to hurt someone or something.

Two strangers, look at us. Neither of us really wants to be here. I know I don't. I don't think he does.

He bites his lip, leans into the curve. Andrea Benodotti. Tanned forearms. Navy Lacoste polo shirt, crocodile watch-strap. He's at least twenty-five – who knows, maybe more? Italian men age slyly – and I'm nineteen, a pale English girl just biting her lip. His hair is dark, oiled, kinked like wool. He smells of the stuff you put in wardrobes to keep moths away. Cedar or something. Or no, maybe it's not that, maybe he just smells of money. Everything he owns is new and expensive. He said so.

'You like it?' he asked me a moment ago.

'What?'

'Eh?'

'Do I like what?' I said.

'This!' He gestured as if it was obvious. 'My car.'

I shrugged. What could I say? A car was a car. He didn't look at me so he didn't see it, the shrug. That's when he lifted his hips up to pull a cigarette out of his pocket, held it in his mouth, pushed in the lighter. After that we didn't speak again.

He doesn't turn to me, his passenger, not once.

Andrea. Sounds like a girl's name, doesn't it? – in England it would be – but no, there's no way this guy is a girl. Girls don't drive with one hand on the wheel while puffing on a cigarette with the other, not on roads like these they don't anyway.

If I glance to my left, then I can see the muscles bunch and slide under the dark skin of his right arm every time he turns the wheel. And this road is swervy and steep, so steep. His jaw is set. Smoke spills through his nose. My stomach counts each separate twist, each violent turn. He knows it. The faster he drives, the more I try not to hold on, not to reach for the dashboard. I don't know where we're going. He hasn't said; I haven't asked. I'm certainly not going to give in and ask.

I try to yawn but realise I'm far too tense. I shut my eyes, desperate for the afternoon to be over. I have to be back by five. But it's only two now. Maybe I should have agreed to see him in the evening, but I have to babysit La Simonetta tonight. These few hours after lunch, siesta time, that's my only time off, my only time for dates.

Though I'm not on this one by choice. It's a blind date – an enforced blind date, very blind indeed.

When my employers realised I was dating a waiter from the Golfo Pizza, they put their foot down.

'There are plenty of nice young men on the island,' Silvana announced, half shocked, half amused. 'La Donatella Benodotti's son for one. He's starting med school in the autumn. He plays bridge and golf. He has an Alfa Romeo. We'll introduce you.'

My pizza waiter had a dusty blue Vespa. He kicked it into life and I held on to his sweaty T-shirt. Halfway down the road it conked out and he had to kick it again, several times, before it restarted. He laughed. The day was hot and bright but the back of his neck smelled of school soap and dark October afternoons.

Andrea and I were introduced at the golf club bar. He shook my hand and his eyes took me in. I had on an old cheesecloth sundress, a bit tatty at the edges. I bit my thumb, annoyed with myself for being there. He asked me if I liked dancing.

I hesitated. I suddenly couldn't remember what I liked.

'Go out on a drive with him at least,' Silvana said when I asked her if I was free that afternoon. 'Then if you get on okay, well maybe he'll take you to the discoteca next time.' Discoteca. She spoke the word with a flicker of barely concealed distaste, as if everyone knew this was all we English *ragazze* wanted – coloured lights and loud music and getting off with boys.

In fact, I hadn't been near a discoteca with my pizza waiter. Instead he'd taken me home to meet his family – la Mamma and three food-smudged baby sisters all smiling up at me in a cramped and steamed-up kitchen. Gloria, Maria and the little one, la Rafaella, who wore a bib with unicorns on it. We ate spaghetti with tomato sauce, Parmigiano grated over it. Rafaella threw her bowl on the floor and my pizza waiter bent and cleared it up.

I dried the dishes for his mamma while he emptied the bin. She told me I was a lovely girl, a *'bellissima ragazza!'*. Afterwards we had a little coffee, which she made on the stove, and then we watched some sport on TV.

Andrea offered me an olive on a stick. I took it. 'Okay,' he said in good and careful English, 'tomorrow. I pick you up here. I take you for nice long drive.'

Down there on the edges of this island, at the warm sandy roots of this place, at sea level, the air's thick enough to brush against your face. You take a small careful breath and straight away it's all over you – lips, tongue, cheeks. It's hot by seven in the morning here, sun pushing and shoving to get through the green slats of the shutters.

But not up here. Up here, it all changes. The trees get closer together, the sea further away and a cool hush falls. On the sharp crook where the road bends, we pass a sudden shepherd with his flock of two or three skinny sheep. He raises a forlorn hand, turns his head to watch us pass. So do the sheep. I smile, too late. Andrea ignores him, drives on. A chill descends and there's a sharp herby smell – of rosemary and thyme, gorse perhaps, then pine. The tall blue-darkness of pine.

I wonder where we're going. I don't think there can possibly be anything up here – not bars, nor discotecas, certainly. A moment ago we passed a small house, set into the hillside among the gorse – *la macchia* – but there's nothing else ahead, just scrub and pine and a road that curves steeply up, on and on and on.

'You like Johnny 'allyday?' Andrea asks me suddenly.

'Who?'

'Johnny 'allyday? English pop guy? You know?'

I shake my head and try to smile. 'I don't know. Don't know him, no.'

He takes a last drag of his cigarette and chucks the stub out of the car. He flicks a look at me and grimaces.

'This is very bad, to do this. Start fire in the – on the – hill.' He throws his head back and laughs for a moment. 'Danger? You know? People in prison for this.' He laughs again, more to himself this time.

The car keeps on going up and up. The air gets colder, darker, and I shiver. The trees pulse past us, fragments of light and dark. It feels like a world in pieces.

Andrea stops the car high up in the centre of the island, in a clearing just off the side of the road. It's even darker and quieter in here. Bracken and pine needles underfoot. So many branches overhead – a roof of darkness – that our voices sound strange, as if we're indoors.

Andrea opens the car door and gets out. Reaches for something in the back of the car.

'Where are we?' My voice sounds small, tired. 'What are we doing here?'

He smiles. He has a blanket, woven brown and pink, a little worn out, in his hands.

'Very beautiful here, yes? Fresh – in this place?' He takes a deep breath, demonstrating.

I blink. Look around me. I can hear stillness, silence. No sound of anything. No bleat of sheep or goat. Not even a breath of wind in the pines.

'It's lovely,' I agree. 'You do know, don't you, that I have to be back by five?'

'Eh?'

I point to my watch. 'Cinque? I must be back.'

Andrea makes a slightly impatient face, clicks his tongue against his teeth.

'We have two hour, yes?'

'Okay. Are we going for a walk or what?'

I'm still sitting in the car, in the passenger side. Andrea comes over and opens my door.

'Come.' His voice is brusque now. 'We sit.'

I get out. He spreads the blanket on the ground. I sit down on it and he sits down too. I pick up a pine cone, press its rough, round shape between my fingers. He reaches out and touches my arm.

*

I only spoke to my pizza waiter in Italian. He had no English, nothing – well, nothing beyond 'hello' and 'how are you?'

He told me I had the most beautiful eyes he had ever seen, sea eyes, *occhi della mare* – he told me he'd seen them change colour at least three times in the half-hour we'd been sitting in the bar.

I laughed. What could I say to that?

He was working so we couldn't talk much, but every time I came to the bar – to get a drink for la Simonetta mostly – he'd make a reason to come over. Was the water okay? Did *la piccola* want some ice? A straw? Some juice – *pera* or *pesca* perhaps?

That's how we got talking about his little sisters – three of them at home. He said they all preferred juice to water. That it drove their mamma *pazza* that they would not drink the plain water from the tap.

I kept my eye on la Simonetta, whose tastes were not of my making. Actually she was an easy child, she liked almost everything. Now she had a bright-coloured wind-mill, red and yellow and silver, and she was waving it around. A white cat had come to play with her. It lay on its back on the warm Golfo paving stones and tried to bat the windmill with its paws. Simonetta stamped her small san-dalled foot and laughed loudly.

My pizza waiter was very quiet, watching her, watching me.

Then he asked if I'd like to go out for an ice cream some time. A *gelato*. 'I could pick you up,' he said, staring at the counter, 'when you get some time off from your work.'

I smiled. I knew it had taken courage for him to ask. I knew he liked me because he wouldn't look at me, not properly, not in the eyes, not once. He always kept his eyes on the floor when we talked.

'Yes please,' I said. 'I'd like that. That would be really nice.'

We made an arrangement to meet up at three.

Beyond him a sweating man in an apron lifted pizzas in and out of the wood oven on a big wooden paddle. In and out, all afternoon. Some of the people on the beach had a very late lunch.

Andrea lights another cigarette, lies back on the rug with his arm behind his head. There's a small sweat patch on the aertex of his polo shirt, under his arm.

'What is it?'

'What's what?'

'What is the matter with you?' he asks me loudly, waving the cigarette in the air.

'What do you mean, what's the matter?' My voice comes out crisper than usual. I hear myself through his ears and think how English I sound, how very foreign and startled.

'You want to – do nothing?'

'No,' I say, 'I don't want to do nothing.'

He gives me another of his impatient looks, then rolls towards me and puts his big brown hand on my breast. I stiffen. His nails are short and clean. I have on a white

T-shirt and a long red cotton skirt, and leather sandals bought in the weekly market in Procchio.

Gently, he squeezes my breast.

'No! What are you doing? Please stop it,' I say, sitting up and pulling away again.

'We make love,' says Andrea as if it were the most obvious thing in the world, and he pushes my red skirt up my legs, my thighs. 'We make love now.'

'No.'

I push his great weight off me and kneel up on the rug, pull all my clothes back down and hug my knees. I'm trembling a little.

'You don't like me?' Andrea spreads his hands in disbelief.

I take a big breath.

'Look, Andrea,' I begin.

My pizza waiter and I walked on the beach in the moonlight. The sand was mottled with shadow. The moon turned the sea navy blue. You could hear the wind in the pines. It was all so perfect that I wondered why I felt disappointed.

He held my hand – so lightly that at times I could hardly feel it. Every time I stole a glance at him I was reminded of how beautiful he was – white face, black hair, black eyes, cheekbones of a statue.

But I knew something was wrong and eventually I worked out what it was. My pizza waiter was far too tentative. In England a man who looked like this would never in a million years be so shy.

I began to wish he would kiss me. In the end we sat on a rock and I tilted my face up and did it to him, the kiss. He didn't hesitate, but when he kissed me back his lips were strangely soft and unconvincing.

'I've never had a girlfriend,' he told me at last.

I stared at him.

'No one. I've never done anything with anyone. You are the first, my first love, *la prima*.'

I shut my eyes and kissed him again. I wondered why he had to be so frank.

When I've made it perfectly clear to Andrea that I am not going to have sex with him right here this afternoon in the pines on the rug, he gets up quickly, pushes me off it, rolls it in a heap and flings it in the back of his car. Alfa Romeo. The name glints at me, tells me what a let-down I am, what a tease.

Andrea jerks his head to show I should get in.

'Last night,' says my pizza waiter when I see him on the beach in the morning, 'I cried about you.'

'Cried about me? But why?

He stares hard at the sand. 'I think I love you.'

I try not to smile. 'You don't mean that,' I tell him gently.

'Oh but I think so. I do. It's been here.' He touches his heart and his eyes are dark, so dark. 'It's been waiting in me a long time.'

I agree to see him after work that night but inside I'm not so sure. I'm going to have to break someone's heart, I tell myself. There's no way round it, that's what will happen. It's the very first time and I guess there's got to be a first time. So that's it. I'm going to have to know for the first time how it feels to have to do it and not care.

On the way back down, driving back towards the sea, Andrea takes the corners as fast as anyone possibly could. Full throttle, like a madman, a man out of his head. My mum would have kittens if she could see. On one corner he hoots loudly and a goat scampers out of the way and down the slope. As we descend, the air grows warmer, thicker. I feel the familiar heat against my face, my chest, my arms.

He doesn't speak; neither do I. What is there, after all, to say? He sucks at the cigarette, then flings it out, so he can put both hands on the wheel, go even faster.

I don't tell him to slow down. I try not to breathe or think or care. I know what he's doing. I know this is my punishment, that this is no more or less than I deserve. I know that this is the kind of thing that happens to girls who refuse one man and break another's heart.

Already I can smell the sea.

The road twists and the car feels as if it might turn over. I don't really care if it does, but still it's with some relief that I finally glimpse the water, a cool, hard slice of turquoise showing through the black branches.

My red skirt is bunched around my knees. I smooth it down, glad of it, glad of everything.

I'm nineteen. I don't know how to behave but that will

come soon enough. Meanwhile, the sea sparkles, waiting for me down there. I've never been in love. All that heartbreak is still out there, in the secret space of the future, waiting for me.

Right now I'm indestructible, an English girl, high up in the centre of the world and on her way down. Coming down a little too fast, perhaps, but you know, I'll be fine. I'm clean, I'm good. And you see, it all waits for me down there – sea, sand, broken hearts. A rinsed-out world. A world of love and hope and disappointments, yes. A world in pieces.

DON REDONDO GOES SURFING
WITH BOB DYLAN

BY CARELESS CONSTIPEDA,
AS TOLD TO
DREW KAMPION

I𝗍 was in my eleventh year at Los Angeles Valley Junior College that one of the most bizarre encounters to date occurred in my long history of bizarre encounters with the Malibu beach bum, Don Redondo.

As some may know, Mr Redondo has been one of the major resources for my ongoing study of the anthropology of the sub-society called surfers.

Why I consider him such a resource is almost a mystery to me now; it seems he was helpful somewhere back there. What's clearer is that I've become a resource to him; I've been taking groceries down to his ticky-tack beach bungalow for eight years now. How that started is a whole other story – best summarised, perhaps, by the phrase 'psycho-physical blackmail'.

Maybe I smoked too many double-enders or something, I don't remember, but the guy had some weird kind of hold on me, that's for sure.

Anyway, going back to this experience in my eleventh year (I'm in my thirteenth now and hope to graduate soon), I was carrying two or three bags of groceries from my car (a '65 Triumph Spitfire) around the side of the house when

I ran into Don. He was pulling his 13-foot rhino-chaser out from under the house. It was dusty and dirty and grangy beyond belief, and I almost warned Don not to tuck it under his arm, but then I noticed that he was dustier and dirtier and grungier than the old surfboard.

'Eh, watchit, where yer goin', Cornflake!' It was a typical unceremonious greeting, peculiar to ageing watermen, I figured.

'Uh, sorry, Don,' I mumbled, though he really irritated me. 'I was just bringing down the groceries.'

'Whatcha think, beagle brain, I ain't got eyes 'n ears? Puttim' behint th' sofer, will ya? I got cump-nee comin'.'

'Why do you want me to put the groceries behind the sofa if you've got company coming, Don Redondo?'

'Cheeze! Ya dumpflake, whatuf he's got yer munchlies or brings a gangle of friends er a hungry date? Ain't got enuf fer one of us let alonely six er nine. So g'wan ahead an stick it back there behint yer sofa and don't be given the Don none a yer Nth degree!'

'Okay, okay . . . sorry I asked.' He certainly wasn't mellowing with time, though he did seem to be fermenting. As I stuffed the bags behind the rancid sofa, I pondered whimsically whether Don might merely be going through a stage. Why couldn't he just become another Malibu bag lady and push a supermarket cart around all day collecting flattened aluminium cans and Slurpee containers? Why couldn't he find a utilitarian niche in the scheme of things and leave me to finish my Associate of Arts degree in relative peace? Why couldn't he just get out of my . . .

These reveries were interrupted by a deep, hollow sound, like someone pounding on an empty oil drum. Don Redondo, as was his custom, had banged me on the head with one of his big, fat, grubby, clenched fists.

'I ast cha whyncha vakkim the floor if yer jest gonna stant there an gawkle?'

'Vacuum the floor?' I asked, taken aback. Don never, ever vacuums his floor. Never ever. He has a vacuum, but he uses it only to get toast out from behind the stove when it falls there, which is rather frequently.

In fact, the one time that I had previously attempted to vacuum the floor for him, he abused me viciously, tirading on about how hard he'd worked tracking in sand all those years to make his home as comfortable as the beach.

And I'll admit he had a point. You could make a sandcastle right there in his living room. You could track a man's footprints through the house. You could cut your feet on glass even. So I was taken aback.

'But, Don,' I said. 'You never, ever vacuum your floor.'

'But, Dahnnn,' he mimicked, 'you nemmer, nemmer vakkim yer floooorrr. Cheeeese! Ain'a guy gotta right ta make 'is own incisions? Ain' I gotta right, hmmm???' He was threatening me with the shovel he uses to pile up the briquettes in his barbecue, so I quickly agreed and went and dragged out the vacuum.

Don grunted a 'humph!' and went out onto the patio. He started putting wax on the old board, and I noticed the ocean beyond him was snot-green and dead flat beneath the thick grey June overcast.

I plugged in the vacuum and switched it on; the incredible rattle and ricochet of billions of sand grains and pebbles and glass up into the machine blocked out even the *zhoom-zhoom* of traffic on the Coast Highway just outside the front door. In fact, the racket was alarming, but I kept at it, mowing the beach on down to the carpet and wondering who was coming to visit.

It took me about an hour to cut a path from the sofa to the sliding glass door. When I got there, I noticed that Don wasn't on the patio any more and that the surfboard was gone. I turned off the machine, slid open the door and stepped out into the blessed silence just in time to see Don Redondo paddle out past the six-inch shorebreak towards an undefined horizon that blended into the squinty light of the grey sky. In fact, it was quite squinty and blinky out there in the indirect light. It felt all cool and hot at the same time. I felt a subtle wave of nausea, a flush of prickly heat, an electric shiver.

I backed up, my head almost beginning to reel, until the backs of my legs touched brick, and I sat down on the barbecue grill. This had always been my power spot, my force-gathering centre, my safe place. This was where Don Redondo had led me through the neoprene ritual. This was the place where my pants got all those black, greasy stripes that I couldn't quite explain to the cleaners on Van Nuys Boulevard. Still, if ever there was a time, now was . . .

A weird howl – a bestial, eerie whoop – caught my head and spun it until I was looking out at sea and seeing Don Redondo dropping over the cornice of a 15-foot wave. He freefell the length of his board, somehow landed on it, made the ugliest fat-assed bottom turn I'd ever seen, and chattered towards the bellowing line of shoulder that was torquing off towards downtown Malibu. I couldn't believe it. The guy was locked into the most incredible California wave I'd ever seen!

As the curl threw over him, Don tried to squat down – though the wave was so big he didn't need to – but his knees wouldn't bend (the old fart's really out of shape, but he's lucky), so he just stooped over and let out another maniacal sound.

'A-hem!' a voice said right by my right ear, scaring my heart into suspended, then irregular, rhythm. 'That cat is really good, huh?"

There was a shortish, thinnish guy about forty standing next to me. He had curly brown hair and splotchy side-burns, the fuzz of a puerile moustache, and dark sun-glasses. He wore a black leather jacket and jeans and low, zip-sided black leather boots. A few of his fingernails were a lot longer than the others. He looked pale, Jewish and familiar. I didn't know what to say, so I nodded, looking back at the ocean. All that was left was a rushing tumble of white water. Don must've been nailed, I thought. Lucky guy. There wasn't another wave in sight.

'Uh, hey man,' the guy said.

'Huh?' I answered, turning back to him.

'Mind if I ask you somethin'?'

'Me?' I said. 'Uh-uh.'

'Why're you sittin' in the barbecue?'

I was searching for the only possible answer that would make me appear sane, but I couldn't find it. Then Don Redondo came sulking up all wet with his rhino-chaser under his arm, and I was off the hook.

'Hey man,' said the little guy to Don.

'Good ja mate it down 'ere,' said the Don. 'There's yer ovational waifs comin' troo. Could be yer day, Bob.'

Bob. That's when it clicked. Bob Dylan! I'd heard he lived at Malibu, at least part of the time, but never really flashed on the possibility that I might actually run into him sometime. And here he was with Don Redondo, of all people! And somehow Don knew him. This was an anthropological, cultural crossover with implications that could blast my research right into the stratosphere. I could possibly get a grant to continue for another eleven years! Maybe I could sell my life story to *Rolling Stone*! Maybe . . .

Excited, I slid out of the barbecue, my mind already working like a well-oiled computer. 'Ah, Mr Dylan, isn't it?' I began, but Don dropped in on me right away.

'This 'ere's my requaintence, Mr Constipashun,' said Don.

'Constipeda,' I interjected. 'Careless, to my friends,' I added.

'Pleased ta meet cha, Mr Constipated,' said Mr Dylan.

'Me too,' I said. 'I was just wondering if—'

'I gotta bort for ya unnerneat th' hooch here,' Don interrupted, leading Mr Dylan around the side of the bungalow. He pulled my 7-foot 6-inch Glenn Kennedy out from under the house and started wiping the dirt off with a wetsuit I kept there with it. This was a shock, too, as I had never seen Don Redondo wipe anything off in my life. 'Star struck,' I muttered as they pushed past me and out to the patio.

Don started telling Dylan the lay of the land, so to speak, the same way he'd told me eleven years earlier – all about sets and paddling and the intricate ways of a waterman. I actually waxed a tad nostalgic hearing it all again. Don hadn't spoken a civil waterman's word of advice to me in years, I suddenly realised.

Dylan took off his boots. He was wearing beige Gucci socks. Then he slipped off his faded blue jeans. Underneath, he wore a pair of electric-yellow Speedos. Then he took off his leather jacket, and there was the same Triumph motorcycle T-shirt he'd worn on the cover of *Highway 61 Revisited*. Either that or Triumph had paid him in T-shirts for the free advertising. Then he took off the T-shirt and I saw what few had seen before: a heart with Joan + Bob tattooed on his left hip. I noticed he was shivering, and I offered him the use of my wetsuit.

'Thanks, kid,' he said. 'Kid' was much better than 'Mr Constipated', I thought. I watched the two of them wax up and then walk out across the beach towards the dead-flat ocean: the huge, grubby, balding, bushy-headed old fart and the thin guy in the baggy wetsuit – he looked like any other surfer from Minnesota except for the sunglasses.

As I watched them paddle out, I couldn't resist the temptation – as an anthropologist – to rifle through Mr Dylan's – Bob's – pockets. Not to steal, just to learn. I found a Hohner Marine Band harmonica (key of A), a Hohner harmonica (key of D), a Hohner harmonica (key of C), a Fender flatpick (light), another pair of sunglasses, a phone number (Valley prefix), two ticket stubs from the Canoga Theater, 37 cents in change, and six $100 bills. I put everything back and left before they'd reached Don's usual line-up (he used an old truck that he'd bolted to the side of the Coast Highway years ago). Maybe I didn't want to see Bob Dylan take gas on a Colony close-out. Maybe I didn't want to see him taking my place in the line-up with Don Redondo. Maybe I just wanted to get out of there before Don found out I hadn't finished the floor (not to mention the ice cream that was melting behind the sofa).

In any case, I was in an unusual mood as I drove slowly down the coast towards Rosa's Cantina. I was craving a massive dose of her patented hot sauce, but I was also looking forward to an afternoon nap. Take time to digest the day's experiences, to—

I had to slam on the brakes to miss hitting the VW bus stopped in front of me. I was almost to the pier and traffic was at a standstill. People were running along the roadside, rushing up from the beach. I thought it must be a landslide or a ten-car crash. People were parking on the road and rushing ahead to see, so I got out and followed them, pressing ahead into the thickening throng.

They were crowding around something. I thought I heard singing, chanting, something with a cadence, but by the time I broke through to the front, the crowd was dispersing right around the crosswalk by the pier. In a moment of panic I wondered if I should rush back and move my car, but just as I turned I saw a man with curly brown hair in a wetsuit walking out onto the pier. He was carrying my surfboard. I rushed after him.

'Mr Dylan!' I called. 'Mr Dylan!' But he wouldn't turn. A group of people passed between us. I lost him. Then I saw him again. He was looking over the railing about halfway out on the pier. I came up quietly, humbly. I didn't know what to say. Then I thought of it.

'Mr Dylan,' I said. 'Did you catch any waves?'

And then he turned to me, and my heart stopped. Completely. I looked carefully. My wetsuit. My surfboard. The same sunglasses.

'Yes?' the man said, taking off the glasses.

'I'm sorry,' I said, backing up. 'I'm ... sorry ... I'm sorry ... I'm sorry ... '

I turned and walked away, back off the pier, my head reeling. It wasn't Bob Dylan at all.

It was Bruce Springsteen!

I reached Coast Highway just in time to see a column of traffic rolling by; there went my '65 Triumph Spitfire. Naturally, Don Redondo was driving. 'Probably heading down to Rosa's,' I thought. He looked at me. He saw me. But he didn't wave. As stupid as Don Redondo sometimes is, he isn't dumb enough to acknowledge that he knows a guy with barbecue stripes on the seat of his pants.

FAMILY HOLIDAY

MIKE GAYLE

DAY 1 – SATURDAY

I'M THIRTY-THREE YEARS OLD and I have never been on a family holiday in the UK. My daughter (henceforward known as The Kid) is fifteen months old and she has never been on a family holiday in the UK, or anywhere else for that matter. My wife (henceforward known as My Wife) is thirty-two years old, has been on plenty of family holidays in the UK and is therefore something of an expert. In her role as accomplished UK holidaymaker, she suggested that we leave the relative comfort of our home in the West Midlands at 10 a.m. rather than as I had suggested 'somewhere reasonably close to the crack of dawn'. I bowed to her greater wisdom, which is why four hours later we find ourselves sitting in a traffic jam just outside of Bristol. This, however, is no ordinary traffic jam. Its head, I suspect, is somewhere in Land's End where a small boy is taking a herd of cows to market, which is holding up the local milkman and thereby causing a knock-on effect that probably finishes somewhere near John O'Groats where a family of five in a Ford Mondeo are on their way to Devon having completely miscalculated how long it takes to cross the entire country by motorway. I kid you not – this traffic jam is so long that it could be spotted from outer space without a telescope (were you to be orbiting the earth in a space shuttle whilst focusing on the M4 just outside of Bristol). To be fair to My Wife, I never in a million years thought that the traffic would be this bad. But then again, I've never been on a family holiday in the UK. And so, as we wait for the small boy with his herd of cows in Land's End to move along the road a bit further, we have no choice but to finish off the last of the Starburst chewy sweets. And we only have two green ones left.

Some time later, having escaped the traffic jam, we find ourselves close to our destination. And though cynical right to my rotten core, I can't help but get excited as we drive along the snaky main road and contemplate our destination: Woolacombe in north Devon. I have heard nothing but good things about Woolacombe. Whenever I mentioned it to friends, the only reaction I ever received was one of amazement and envy. 'Oooh, Woolacombe,' they would say. 'You'll love it.' And as spending over a thousand pounds on a holiday that doesn't involve air travel intrinsically makes me miserable, it had better be everything they say it is.

As we turn a sharp corner – like the flick of a switch, the madness of the motorway is forgotten – I can now see the sea. There's no doubt about it. There it is sandwiched in our vista between the sky and a couple of dodgy-looking guesthouses. My Wife tells me that once you see the sea you finally feel like you're on holiday. I look at her with genuine love in my eyes, and can't help but think that she's completely insane. Regardless, seeing the sea does bring some cheer to my heart, and whether I like it or not, the holiday has begun.

DAY 2 – SUNDAY

Even though The Kid is only fifteen months old, we have spent all morning explaining the concept of the beach. 'It's a place where there's lots of sand,' says My Wife. The Kid looks at her blankly. 'And because there's lots of sand, you'll need a bucket and spade.' The Kid looks at the bucket and spade blankly then looks back at My Wife. 'And then there's the sea,' continues My Wife. 'It's like a gigantic cold bath only it's green.' At this The Kid looks at me with a worried look on her face as if to ask the question: Are you hearing what I'm hearing? I shrug as if to say: I hear what you're hearing but not even I can save you. With that she escapes to her bedroom and closes the door behind her. 'It's not scary,' yells My Wife through the door. 'It's fun!' Though I can't see my daughter's face, my guess is she isn't convinced because she still refuses to come out. My Wife just rolls her eyes to the Artexed ceiling, sighs and informs me that she's going to have a shower.

Ten minutes later and we're all ready to make our first journey to the beach as a family. I am wearing a T-shirt and shorts and trainers, My Wife is wearing similar, and our daughter is sporting a rather natty bathing costume combined with multicoloured jelly shoes. I suspect she loves these shoes more than she loves me. She smiles at them and talks to them as we load up the pram with all the essentials for a day at the beach (three towels, two changes of clothes, kids' sun lotion, adult sun lotion, a copy of the *Guardian*, two novels, five ordinary nappies, three 'swim' nappies, two mobile phones, nappy sacks, a beach ball and a bucket and spade).

'Are you ready for the beach?' I ask The Kid joyfully.

She stops smiling at her jelly shoes and once again looks worried.

'Well, if you're not, it's too late now,' I say in reply to her doleful expression. And before she can make a run for it I scoop her up and strap her into her pram.

As we make our way along the main road from the hotel we are joined by other holidaying families. I can't help but look at these other families and compare them to my own. Most have more children than we do. Their children also appear to be older than mine (mostly in the seven-to-eleven age bracket). All of them without exception appear to be dressed in wetsuits.

'When did wetsuits become fashion wear?' I ask My Wife.

'I don't know,' she replies. 'Maybe people don't like getting wet any more.'

'But that's the whole point of wetsuits,' I say knowledgeably. 'Water comes through them and they get wet. Otherwise they'd be called dry suits.'

'If you know so much about wetsuits,' spits My Wife,

'then why are you asking me stupid questions about them?'

I shrug. 'Shall we just go to the park instead?'

My Wife nods and my daughter laughs gaily at her jelly shoes.

DAY 3 – MONDAY

It's a new day and we're finally heading back to the beach again, but now we know why everyone in Woolacombe from postal operatives to the woman behind the counter in Londis is wearing a wetsuit. Unbeknownst to us, my family and I are holidaying in the second city of surfing in the UK.

'What's the first?' I had asked a woman standing on a street corner yesterday on the way back from the park. (She'd offered to tattoo a dragon on my back in semi-permanent henna for £3.50 and seemed to have time on her hands to talk.)

'Newquay,' she replied.

'So Woolacombe is like the Birmingham of surfing?'

'I suppose,' she said, looking perplexed. 'Only without a spaghetti junction.'

'Cheers,' I replied.

'What about the dragon?' she asked.

I looked at the design again. It looked less like a mythical fire-breathing emblem of Welsh-ness and more like a mange-ridden dog contorting its hind legs to scratch behind its ears.

'I think I'll need to think about it,' I lied.

Fortunately today we don't see her. Thus I don't have to feign an allergy to both henna and badly drawn dragons. When we eventually reach the turning for the beach, I take one step round the corner and stop in my tracks. I have never (and I do mean never) seen so many people packed onto such a small amount of sand in my entire life. It's like attending a Glastonbury festival dedicated to sea worship. I can barely see the sand amongst the neoprene-wetsuit-clad bodies.

'I don't understand,' I say to My Wife. 'What's going on?'

'Nothing's "going on",' she snaps. 'This is what summer in England is like.'

With great difficulty we drag our 'all-terrain urban child travel system' (aka a pushchair) across the sand.

'They lied,' I say to My Wife as once again the pushchair (minus child now being carried by its mother) became stuck in a deep furrow of sand of its own making. 'It's not all-terrain at all.'

'I expect when they called it that they weren't expecting many bedouins to be testing out their claims,' replies My Wife.

'But it says "all-terrain",' I say, reading the fancy lettering on the pushchair's chunky tyres. 'Surely "all-terrain" should mean just that – "all-terrain"? Surely if they didn't mean "all-terrain" they should have been legally obliged to call it "some-terrain", or at the very least "all-terrain-apart-from-sand-terrain", because "all-terrain" by my way of thinking should include sand. Don't you think?'

I don't get a reply from My Wife because she has grown tired of my ceaseless moaning and has upped her pace considerably. My Wife and The Kid are now mere pinpricks in the distance. By the time I catch up with them they have managed to locate the only patch of sand for miles that hasn't already been colonised. The space is sandwiched between a middle-aged couple and their three teenage boys, a young couple and their two young daughters, and two teenage boys who appeared to be unsupervised. All of the people surrounding us have two things in common: the now seemingly ubiquitous wetsuits, and strange colourful tent-like constructions. I looked around me and noticed for the first time that of the quarter of a million people on the beach we are the only ones without a beach tent.

'Did we miss the memo?' I ask My Wife as we settle ourselves down on our suddenly outdated beach towels. 'When did it become obligatory to surf and camp at the same time? Did they have these things when you used to go on holiday?'

'No,' says My Wife looking up at the scorching sun, 'but they seem like a good idea.' She pauses, not looking at me. I know what this pause means. It means one of us is going to have to return to civilisation and purchase one of the aforementioned beach tents. And that one of us is going to be me.

'Shall I take the all-terrain pushchair with me just in case it's too heavy?' I ask.

My Wife doesn't reply. She just sighs and smiles at the

same time – a seemingly impossible action she has perfected in the time we've been together – and so I kiss her and The Kid goodbye and utter the famous last words, 'I may be some time.' I must make for a pitiful sight because I've only travelled a few steps when My Wife calls after me, 'Hold on, we're coming too.'

Though we buy the beach tent, we've lost our enthusiasm for the beach, and so we spend the rest of the day in the park followed by an afternoon by the hotel pool.

DAY 4 – TUESDAY

Today we're going exploring. It's not enough to sit on a beach and stare at the same sea we stared at the day before. We need to sit on a different beach and stare at a different sea. To this end we have decided to go to nearby Ilfracombe for the day. We imagine that as Ilfracombe sounds an awful lot like Woolacombe they will be pretty much the same. In fact, such is my imagination that as we begin driving towards our destination in the pouring rain, I am hoping that Ilfracombe is so much better than Woolacombe that it has its own weather system. 'Due to freak atmospheric conditions,' reads my imaginary guide to north Devon, 'Ilfracombe has an unusually warm climate similar to what one might find on the French Riviera. In fact, locals often refer to it as "the English Monte Carlo".' As we pull up in Ilfracombe town car park – a car park so steep that small goats were unable to keep their footing and were tumbling down the hill past us – it occurs to me that my ever hopeful imagination is in for yet another kicking. Locals are about as likely to refer to their town as 'the English Monte Carlo' as Milton Keynes is likely to refer to itself as 'the new Provence'. I have never in my life been to such a depressingly grey town. It's not just the rain either. The grey actually feels like it's in the air. Descending the heights of Ilfracombe car park without the aid of a Sherpa, the three of us head through the town centre towards the seafront, reasoning that that might be where the action is because it certainly isn't here. Ilfracombe town centre appears to have been frozen in time somewhere around 1953. Not only were there charity shops for causes long since forgotten (Palsy Research anyone?) but some of the items they sold were so of their time that no amount of ironic fashion sense could have saved them.

'Look at this!' exclaimed My Wife, pointing to a cushion with a startlingly vivid colour picture of a kitten on it. 'It's hideous.'

Everyone in the charity shop ('Collecting money for the League Against Black Death since 1512') turned and stared at us intently so we swiftly made our exit.

With the shop behind us we made our way to Ilfracombe harbour and were pleasantly surprised by how picturesque it was compared to the rest of the town. On one side of the harbour there were fishing boats bobbing up and down, barnacle-encrusted ropes dangling into the water and all of it set against the magnificent backdrop of the granite rock face of the upper part of the town. On the other side were yet more boats, a party of school children being taught to canoe and, of course, the open sea. Hoping that the harbour was setting the standard for the rest of Ilfracombe, we headed towards the seafront.

The first sign that we were back to the Ilfracombe of 1953 was the ancient merry-go-round that looked like it had dropped straight out of a Scooby Doo cartoon. The second sign was the seafront itself. It looked tired. It looked exhausted. It looked like it needed putting out of its misery. The third sign was that Pam Ayres was supposed to be playing at the town's theatre soon.

'This is why Woolacombe's gone surfing crazy,' says My Wife as we sit down to eat our packed lunch on the benches overlooking the kind of seascape that wouldn't have looked out of place in *The Perfect Storm*.

'I suppose,' I reply, looking at The Kid who, like My Wife, is surveying the row of pound shops, chip shops and general tat shops behind us sadly. I suddenly felt sorry for Ilfracombe, as if it were a Cinderella that had never been taken to the ball. 'All it needs is a bit of love and attention,' I say as it begins to rain harder, 'and it wouldn't seem half as bad.'

'Hmm,' says My Wife, chewing on a cheese and pickle sandwich. 'I suppose so.'

'Maybe it's nicer in the sunshine,' I say hopefully.

She doesn't reply, which in My Wife's non-verbal lexicon means let's agree to disagree.

DAY 5 – WEDNESDAY

'What do you want to do today?' asks My Wife as I study the *A–Z of Devon and Cornwall*.

'I want to go here,' I say, pointing to the map.

Intrigued, My Wife and The Kid approach me hoping that I'm pointing to somewhere that has proper shops and a fresh supply of Sun Maid raisins.

'Padstow?' says My Wife.

'Yeah,' I reply.

'Why?'

I think for a moment. 'Because I've heard of it so it must be good.'

My Wife takes the map from me. 'It's miles away,' she says. 'We wouldn't get there until midday.'

I look at the map again, following the A39 from Bideford on page twenty-seven through to Padstow on page eighteen. She's right. It is miles away.

'How about Bude?' she says.

'I've never heard of Bude,' I tell her.

'It's on the way to Padstow,' she replies, pointing to page seventeen.

'What's there?' I ask.

'I don't know,' she replies.

'Fair enough,' I say cheerfully. 'Let's go to Bude.'

It strikes me, as once again we load up the car with provisions and our sole child, that a lot of the decisions My Wife and I make in life are like the one we've just made about Bude. There's a beautiful sort of randomness about the way we go about things that I find quite heartwarming. We're going to Bude. But we don't really know why we're going to Bude, apart from the fact that it's closer to where we are now than Padstow. And even though we know that being on the way to Padstow doesn't necessarily mean that Bude will have any similarity to it (see Ilfracombe), somehow it all makes sense.

It's soon clear that driving to Padstow and back again in a day would've been sheer madness because Bude is miles away. We don't actually arrive there until after midday, by which time The Kid is so hungry she's started gnawing on her own fists. We follow the main road into the town and then follow signs out the other side pointing us in the direction of Crooklets beach. Soon we find ourselves in a large car park overlooking a grassy bank that's home to an alternative makeshift car park that is fifty pence cheaper if you stay the entire day. It's raining again and the sky has turned slate grey. And The Kid is screaming at the top of her lungs to let us know that she's ravenous. I feel depressed. My Wife dashes out of the car to the boot to get The Kid's lunch and gets soaked in the process. While our child inhales her sandwiches, My Wife and I sit in silence watching the windscreen steam up.

The rain stops some ten minutes later and so, with The Kid now sated, we decide to get out of the car. As we clamber out onto the damp tarmac we can hear the sound of crashing waves, though we can't see the sea. A few moments later and we're there. Crooklets beach is nothing like Woolacombe Sands. To my mind it seems more raw.

More natural. Probably more suited to moments of reflection in a cagoule than ball games in neoprene wetsuits. There are a handful of holidaymakers on the beach. People who must have remained on the sand through the rain. I can't help but admire the spirit of a person who defies British weather so wilfully. I can imagine them railing to the skies with clenched fists held aloft, 'We'll have fun on the beach no matter what you throw at us!' My Wife and I, however, are not this sort of people. We're warm-cups-of-tea-and-poloneck-jumper people. Plus we both wear glasses and for us rain is our kryptonite. The beach today definitely wouldn't work for us. Plus The Kid – who usually races everywhere like a demented greyhound – decides that her legs are no longer working and insists that we carry her. The only plan we'd had was to do what we'd have done if we'd stayed in Woolacombe: sit on the beach in our brand-new beach tent and convince ourselves that we were having less fun than everyone else.

'What shall we do now?' asks My Wife, buckling under the weight of our child.

'Let's go for a walk,' I say, taking charge.

And we do just that. Taking it in turns to carry The Kid, we follow the coastal path to nearby Summerleaze beach. As we walk and talk, we take in the bracing sea air and drink in the views. Even though it's August it feels like November but this enhances our walk rather than detracts from it. We wouldn't be caught dead walking on an English beach in real November for fear of freezing to death. This way we get to imagine what it might be like, get the healthy outdoor glow we often envy in ramblers, while never actually risking frostbite.

DAY 6 – THURSDAY

Not only is today the final full day of our holiday. Not only are we not travelling anywhere. More importantly than any of these facts: today, the sun is back. The mini-winter is over. It's officially summer again.

'Look at that,' I say to My Wife, pointing to the sky. 'It's the sun.'

'Hmm,' says My Wife, who is making The Kid breakfast.

'I think we should spend the whole day today on the beach,' I continue. 'We should take books and magazines to read, a small picnic to cover lunchtime and those times when you just feel peckish and . . . ' At this point I pause to focus my attention on my daughter, who is for reasons known only to herself currently licking the TV screen. 'And you can make a sandcastle.'

The Kid stares at me for a few moments as though she finds me mildly amusing and then returns to licking the TV.

'Sandcastles,' I repeat.

'Mmmm,' she says kissing the TV. 'Mmmm.'

I must admit I am somewhat obsessed with sandcastles. But in a good way. To me the sandcastle is the perfect symbol of a happy childhood. What is after all a childhood without sandcastles? A something-hood, yes. But a *child*hood?

No. Children need sandcastles. And there's no way that I'm going to be responsible for my only child appearing on *Trisha* one day as an adult to tell the story of how she always felt there was something missing from her life. She will have her sandcastle. And she will like it. Today, I tell myself, no matter what happens, we shall make it to the beach and stay there all day.

The first problem we have to overcome on reaching the beach is the fact that The Kid has an acute fear of sand. Despite having spent ten minutes on Monday sitting on a beach towel, My Wife and I hadn't noticed that The Kid hadn't set foot on a grain of sand the whole holiday. It's only now, having found our own square metre of beach on which to set up camp, that we realise that The Kid is so scared of sand that she's standing on one leg on tiptoe with a look of complete terror on her face. It appears to be a similar phobia to the acute fear of grass she had a while ago, which she only conquered when we left her in the middle of our lawn and ran away. (My Wife has convinced me that we'll be paying through the nose for therapy for her over this incident for the rest of our lives.)

'She hates the sand,' says My Wife.

'Mmmm,' says The Kid, still standing on one leg.

'How can anyone hate the sand?' I ask, bending down to rescue her. I take her in my arms and sit down in the beach tent. Then I pick up a handful of sand to show her. 'Look,' I tell her as the sand runs through my fingers. 'It's fun.'

'No,' she says firmly, which word has the accolade of being not only the first one she ever learned but also the only one she ever uses. 'No.'

'But it's just—'

'No.'

'But it's just—'

'No.'

'But it's just—'

'No.'

'But it's just—'

'No.'

'But it's just—'

'No.'

'But it's just—'

'No.'

At this point in the battle of wills My Wife steps in. 'You have to show her that it's fun,' she explains slowly. 'Then she'll come round to it.'

'Fun?' I say. 'I can do fun.'

And so I take out the bucket and spade and begin digging deep into the surrounding sand to get the moist stuff that is perfect for castle-making. Within seconds The Kid is peering over my shoulder, intrigued. I offer her a go with the spade.

'No,' she says once again, but still she stares.

I fill the bucket with sand and then pat the contents firmly in. The Kid grabs my arm to get a better look at the patting. She smiles. I can see that she likes the patting but she still seems wary. I take the sand-filled bucket and turn it upside down. Two sharp taps on the base and then I slowly pull the bucket up, revealing the first sandcastle I've made in sixteen years. It's hard to say which of us is more overjoyed. We sit and stare in wonder, my daughter and I, at this magnificent creation, and in that moment everything crystallises. This is what holidays in England are about. This is why people like to be beside the seaside, beside the sea. It's all about sandcastles.

JOURNEY TO THE SEA

LIBBY PURVES

'THERE'S NO REASON,' SAID THE doctor carefully, 'that you shouldn't stay as active as possible.'

No reason? said the high, furious voice inside Julia's head. No reason? A death sentence, isn't that a reason? Aloud, though, she said nothing. She had never made scenes, and despised women who did. The doctor, who was sandy-haired and a little pudgy, shifted uneasily in his chair, so that she realised how young he was; she felt a flash of pity for him and resolved to say something. But before the silence could deepen he recovered his poise and went on, his voice professionally kind and level.

'Walking is good. Probably not cycling, as you might find your balance a bit affected by the medication. But swimming – swimming is good. In a lifeguarded pool, obviously. The faintness, otherwise . . . ' He tailed off, numbed by her silence.

'Swimming,' repeated Julia. She found she now had a surprising desire to help the poor boy, and gave a sudden radiant smile that startled rather than reassured him. 'Yes, I live just across from the leisure centre. Never been in there. Haven't swum for years. But I see them coming out with towels.'

'There!' said the doctor, almost as relieved as if he had offered her a certain cure. 'That might do you very well. The medication has a much better chance if you're active. Keep the – er – blood flowing.'

Julia passed out through the electric doors of the hospital into a new world, its colours brighter and its human noises louder than ever before. A mother pushed a baby past in a humbug-striped buggy and its small face was soft and bright as a flower; an old man, older than Julia would ever be, hobbled past and his gait seemed almost a dance. She closed her eyes, shook her head violently, then looked down the road at the happy riot of cars and lorries, hearing with incredulity the vivid hum of life. In two years – maybe less, not likely more – she would be dead. The doctors had said so. The tests were incontrovertible. This thing in her bones was too deep for excision, too rampant to be held off for long with chemicals. They had not wanted to tell her while she was alone, knowing that she lived by herself, but Julia had insisted. Thirty years of widowhood, she said tartly, had taught her to deal with matters of all kinds without imposing on other people. Even now, confronted with the need to inform the office manager and alert Human Resources to her plight, she shrank from the duty. Her coming death, surely, was her own business. The dark would come, and then whatever lay beyond the dark – Julia was not without vague unexamined religious belief. But to discuss the darkness, and what to do with the months before it came, was an additional embarrassment that Julia saw no need to court. Not yet, anyway. If timor mortis came over her later on, or if she couldn't look after herself even before the hospice stage, she would tell Sally and Jack or perhaps her cousin Catherine. But there was no need to trouble them with it now, and endure up to two years of pity. If she had had children, now, that would be different; they would need to be prepared. But she and Joe had had no children. A blessing, really.

'It won't be much of a funeral,' she said, aloud but under her breath; she was walking homeward now past the Odeon, heading for the 1930s red-brick block where she and Joe had thought themselves so lucky to find a corner flat. And: 'Oh, I'd better make a proper will.' It still seemed incredible, as she walked with long strides in her flat sensible shoes, that this efficient body would soon be still and silent. At the gate of the flats she felt suddenly reluctant to go in, but having eaten nothing for breakfast, on hospital instructions, she was hungry and thirsty. Glancing across the road to the council leisure centre, she remembered that Sally had told her the café there was good.

She crossed the road, not bothering to look around her – what need, now? As soon a lorry as a hospice – and went in. While she waited for her tea and scone, standing by the Formica counter, she picked up a flyer. All her life, Julia had been unable to wait without reading something, even if it was only a safety notice or a railway ticket. And this, at least, had an intriguing headline:

SWIM TO HOLLAND!

Get fit and see Europe! Swim the equivalent distance of the sea crossing from Harwich to the Hook of Holland, all within your safe and friendly local pool, and ferry operators Nordseespeed will give you a FREE return foot-passenger ticket from Harwich. And to complete your well-earned minibreak, our healthy-living sponsors Instabran will throw in a free return train ticket to Amsterdam.

[185 km or 100 nautical miles is 7,400 lengths.]

The café was empty. The girl on the counter pushed her tea across, slopping a little into the saucer.

'What's all this?' said Julia, tapping the flyer. 'Are people really going to swim 7,400 lengths?'

'Ooh yeah,' said the girl. 'We've given out loads of record cards. They have to be signed off, see, every time you come and do your lengths. My boyfriend's up to 840, I've got nearly 300; it's amazing how they build up.'

'But the fare's not much anyway, not for foot passengers,' protested Julia, noticing with relief the way that this ordinary conversation was somehow shrinking the cold, hard knot of despair in her stomach. 'And it costs about two pounds to swim, so if you came – what – about three hundred times, to do twenty lengths or whatever, you'd have spent £600 – for a thirty-quid ticket.'

'There's concessions,' said the girl rather haughtily. 'And anyway, it's a sort of game, innit? Makes you want to get the lengths in. Health, an' that.'

Julia took the flyer with her, and gazed down at it while she drank her tea and brushed the crumbs off the lapels of her dull sensible jacket. Active, she thought. The doctor said I should swim. Perhaps I'll swim to Holland, or sink in the attempt. Carrying her plate back, noticing that the girl at the counter still seemed a little distant in response to her earlier brusqueness, she waved the flyer again and said: 'I think I'll do it, you know. You're right, it's a game. My husband would have liked the idea.'

'Thass nice,' said the girl, mollified.

'He loved the sea, you see,' said Julia. 'Joe always used to say that when we got a bit richer we'd get a boat and sail across the North Sea. He used to read those children's books. Arthur Ransome, I think it was.'

'Lovelee,' said the girl. 'D'you want a record card then? Only they're at the main desk now, we've run out.'

Two days later, on the far side of several nightmares and an embarrassing, pity-laden interview with Human Resources, Julia came back. She had, with customary thoroughness, made a study of the public swimming times and identified seven to nine in the morning and eight to nine in the evening as the most congenial opportunity: over-16s only, strictly lane swimming. Lowering herself into the soup-warm water in her frumpish costume she shuddered a little, breathing in the scent of chlorine, contemplating the idea of 7,400 lengths with little enthusiasm. But the water upheld her – she had forgotten how comforting, how womblike was that feeling, how pleasant to feel the middle-aged flabbiness of one's breasts and midriff being surrounded and supported by the uncritical element. After a few tentative strokes she found her legs remembering the shape of kicks and her cupped hands grasping at the water ahead of her. Breaststroke, crawl – ah yes, and that comforting sidestroke her father had taught her. And back-stroke, yes. Two ways to do it. Either with the arms wind-milling high and fast, or just flapping gently at her side.

She did a length in each style, making five; a little out of breath, she clung to the rail, keeping apart from the fast swimmers who made a swishing turn and powered off to the far end in half her time. Blinking water from her sting-ing eyes, she resolved to get goggles. Because she now knew for certain that this would go on. Yes, it would go on. 'To the very brink,' she muttered to herself as she padded to the changing room and got her card stamped for fifteen lengths. She would swim this virtual North Sea, morning and evening, and win her right to cross the real one. No Charon for her, demanding coin and setting Cerberus growling. She would swim her own Styx, at her own speed.

'Feeling comfortable?' said the pudgy young doctor a fort-night later. 'Sleeping well?'

'Yes,' said Julia, surprised at herself. 'I didn't at first. I had nightmares. But now I go swimming in the evening, and it tires me out.'

'Jolly good.'

There seemed nothing else to be said between them, but as she reached the door Julia turned and said, 'I'm only three miles out, of course. Nautical miles. But it means I'm in among the approach channel buoys now.' Not pausing to see his astonished face, she left, almost laughing. She was having tea with Sally later when she enlarged on this theme.

'I'm really looking forward to the East Shipwash, and when I get to the Inner Gabbard I'll feel I've achieved something.'

'Where did you get the map?' asked Sally, who – still in ignorance of the reason for it – had been following her friend's theoretical adventure with incredulous amusement. She gestured to the kitchen wall in the little flat, where a blue-and-green nautical chart was pinned up and showed a few small black Xs in the bottom left-hand corner. 'It looks like a proper big ship chart.'

'It is. I went to a chandlery place, where Joe used to go and look wistfully at all the boat stuff,' said Julia. 'It's quite interesting. I got a booklet to go with it because I didn't understand the abbreviations. You'd think the sea was just empty, but there are all these buoys and lightships and things, and marks about how deep the bottom is. When I get to about three thousand lengths I'll be in a busy shipping channel, quite dangerous, actually. Then at 7,440 lengths exactly, I'll probably swim just about underneath the Maas West oil platform.'

'You're bats,' said Sally. 'If you want to go on the ferry, the foot-passenger ticket only costs about thirty quid. I'll come with you. We'll do a weekend and go to the Van Gogh museum. No need to turn into a prune trying to swim it.'

'I want to,' said Julia. 'We all do. There are quite a few of us, you know, queuing up at that desk every evening to declare our lengths. We get quite competitive.'

'How many can you do at one go?'

'I topped out at forty lengths. That's a kilometre. Some of them go on for ages and do about sixty, but I get tired – the drugs—' Julia broke off and moved on hastily to safer ground, mortified at having nearly told her friend the truth. 'I mean, for my asthma. But I think it does me good. Umm – have you seen much of your boys lately? How did Adam's job interview go?'

As the weeks went by, the swimming sessions took on ever more importance, growing longer as Julia's stamina increased. Morning and evening were no longer enough. After three months, just as she was approaching the shipping separation channel in the Noord Hinder Precautionary Area, Julia went to Human Resources and invoked her right to invalidity leave.

'I can't tell you how sorry we are to lose you,' said the HR chief. 'But you must do whatever's best. You're actually . . . ' He hesitated, noting the thinning of her hair. 'Looking rather well, considering.'

'I take exercise,' said Julia briefly. 'Anyway, I've left a long handover document. Eleanor has it.'

Walking away from the last job of her life, she reflected in the lift, would seem more sombre and momentous a parting if it were not for the possibility that tonight she would almost definitely be level with the Noord Hinder

Racon. It was only another half a nautical mile, thirty-five lengths. She was well over halfway across now. After long, blank blue weeks of keeping the faith and watching the pencil marks crawl across the kitchen chart, she would soon be out of the emptiness of mid-ocean and back in the shallow water, in among the winking channel buoys, kicking and squirming through warm chlorine and imaginary salt waves towards Hoek van Holland and the edge of a new world.

'O my America, my new found land,' she murmured. Joe used to quote Donne to her when they were first married, innocents tasting with incredulous joy the secure pleasures of bedtime. She had only five years with him before the accident and had lived thirty years since, each year more senior at work and sensible at home, more grown-up and reasonable and responsible and lonely. Why had she forgotten the dreams they had together? Why had she not followed them? Taken sailing lessons, travelled, signed up for one of those alarming round-the-world adventures that other middle-aged women were always doing in the newspapers.

'Didn't want to, I suppose,' she said aloud. 'He had the dreams. I just followed on. Well, Joe' – she was at the door of the swimming pool now, holding the towel bag without which she never left home – 'I'm coming now. Another fifteen miles.' The assistant on the front desk knew her, and her increasingly noticeable habit of talking to herself. She smiled in professional welcome.

'Fifteen miles, did you say? Getting close!'

'Yes. Has anybody got all the way yet?'

'Mr Blakemore. He was first. Oooh, he was pleased. He went over with his wife last weekend. Apparently it was ever so rough.'

'I shan't mind.'

'You could always leave it till spring. There isn't a time limit, is there?'

'I don't want to wait. I want to cross the North Sea and look out and know that I swam all that distance. I swam it!'

Julia put down her money, reflecting that as from next week she would get in for 70p as 'unwaged' and that it was surprising how little she minded that indignity. Minutes later, limbs heavy and heart light, she was swimming slowly under the bright neon, alone in her roped-off lane, and the water heaved with her dizzy breathlessness and seemed already salt in her eyes.

On the edge of the pool the young lifeguard watched her; incurious, magnificent in his strong young body. It was his gap year, and he was serving his time in this job to pay for his travels. The slow-moving, earnest old woman in the baggy costume might have been from a different species. Keen-eyed under the bright lights, the boy saw very little.

THE NAIAD

SARAH WHITELEY

M Y JOURNEY TO THE SEA began when I was tiny. My mum, who used to surf in the 1960s, would sit me on one of her old boards and push me into the little breakers in about six inches of water, and we both soon realised I had an insatiable appetite for the waves, an appetite that has never really gone away. We moved to Saunton in Devon when I was nine, and from then on I'd quite literally roll down the garden into the sea: living on the beach is something you never take for granted if you surf, and opening the curtains in the morning to the sea, long perfect lines of swell rolling into the bay creating beautiful peeling waves, still has the same effect on me now as it did then.

Learning to surf in Saunton Sands in the late 1980s was great. The boys were surfing with their nine-foot-plus longboards, and the atmosphere was mellow, and being the only girl in the water never bothered me because I've always been a tomboy, forever trying to keep up with an elder brother who was exceptionally good at sports. So there I was, a tiny whippersnapper, itching to better my surfing and loving every minute that I spent in the water; watching other surfers and looking out for new moves. I was surfing four times a day in the summer holidays, before school and after school through the winter months in temperatures of as low as 7 degrees. French, English or Keen As – yes, I was mustarded right up. And I just couldn't get enough of the sea – it draws you in, and when that happens your life completely changes.

And then things started to get competitive. I was tackling more challenging waves, faster, more powerful and more dangerous, but I was gaining confidence and building up my experience, and it was really satisfying seeing myself improving. And that's when the boys started to notice me, and they weren't too sure how to handle it. They seemed to think along the lines of: 'She's only a girl – she won't make the wave, so I'll catch it and it won't be wasted.' And I realised it was going to take some time to convince this new set of wave warriors that girls can hold their own in the waves. But over time, and after a few tricky moments, I made some good friends and mutual respect blossomed, which felt really good. And when I started pulling off some good moves on my surfboard and throwing a bit of spray on the waves, they started to take me seriously and give me a bit of credit, so that by the time I was going out when the surf was really big, they would help me out by shouting me into waves. They knew I wasn't messing about and that I was going for it out there.

And then things started to get really interesting. When I was sixteen, Tim Heyland, from a local surf shop, barked at me in his army corporal voice: 'Oi, Whiteley, English

Nationals, Woolacombe, if you come in the top three I'll sponsor you.' And since I reckoned I had nothing to lose, I gave it a try. And I won, much to my surprise, and that was the start of my competition career, and I entered every national surfing competition over the next ten years. Contest surfing can be extremely frustrating, since you can never guarantee waves at a certain time on a certain day, and there's vast amounts of waiting, hanging around for your heats. I've spent many an hour feeling increasingly queasy, sitting in damp clothes trying to focus beyond the windscreen wipers and steamy glass. And then the next morning it's back to work and back to training, which usually involved a soft sand run up the beach, followed by a severe beating of a punch bag and a painful medley of sit-ups. Maybe a paddle to Croyde on my longboard if the surf was flat, but usually I'd be surfing come rain or shine, through huge and mini waves, and the odd gale.

One of my happiest achievements was winning the Junior European Championships in Portugal when I was eighteen, followed by winning the biggest grin award too. I was on the British team twice for the World Championships, and team trips like those are fantastic to be involved with. There were three of us who would regularly make most of the finals, so we had a healthy amount of rivalry and in turn we each had a slice of the winner's cake. In the early days the standard of women's surfing was pretty average, but these days there are some tremendous women surfers around, and we're definitely not just sitting on the beach in our bikinis watching the boys any more; we're out there doing it, and catching up rapidly. Especially with the likes of Layne Beachley around, six times and current world champion, to name but one. My personal favourite was Lisa Anderson for the US, who was one of the most influential female surfers to take the standard to the next level, and she notched up five world titles along the way. And Robyn Davies, our home-grown talent from Helston, Cornwall, has been putting in some impressive performances, battling it out with the pros on the WQS tour (World Qualifying Series).

Surfing has taken me to some amazing places: Indonesia, Hawaii, Fiji, Sri Lanka and the States, to mention a few, and I always spent the bulk of the winter in Manly, Sydney. One trip that sticks out was to New Zealand. I cannot describe how stunning this country is, so diverse: lush rainforests, crispy beaches, silent mountains. The place is tops, and the people are too. Another hot spot would have to be Ireland. Uncrowded surf, Guinness, seafood chowder, Irish bread. Perfect. And Fuerteventura has turned into another haunt; there are some great waves to be had along the north track, point after point of perfect rollers. And the Maldives were pretty amazing too, where the most wonderful waves peel past the tiny atoll of Lohifushi. On one particular occasion the surf had picked up and the other residents of the island had scarpered from the water, except for one longboarder called Brian from Salcombe in south Devon, and me. And I remember catching some of the best waves of my life, in the most beautiful surroundings, translucent sea, wearing only board shorts and a rash vest. Heaven. And Fiji is pretty extraordinary as well, although the rips were really hard work when we were surfing the outer islands. Paddling back out to catch wave after wave seemed to take for ever as the current keeps pulling you back in the opposite direction, but I don't think I'll ever forget the colour of the sea there. It transfixes you; it's got to be the most beautiful blue in the world.

During my competition years I was lucky enough to be involved with Surfers Against Sewage, a charity set up by Chris Hines and a few other surfers who were fed up going surfing in filthy waters, coming out with sore throats and bad stomachs. Their aim is to clean up our seas to benefit all water users, and for four years I went on the tour bus they organised, travelling around Great Britain to a different place each day, with press calls and other media activities, school talks and fundraisers, and we met some great people along the way.

And now for the first time in my life I don't want to run away to other shores. I've set up a surf school with my partner, based at Saunton Sands where I learnt to surf, and I've got a whole new perspective; I'm not just surfing for myself any more. When you start teaching something, you have to learn yourself again. Everything you have been doing instinctively for the last fifteen years has now got to be explained in great detail, and it gets fairly technical in parts. But it's been fantastic introducing so many people to the sport, and it's even better when you get to see their big smiles when they stand up for the first time and ride a wave into the shore. It gives me huge satisfaction. And last summer I was involved in a girls-only coaching club, and as word got around we had thirty local girls out there, loving every minute of it, which was brilliant. The club was free, and the idea was to get more women involved in the sport. We'd help coach them and give them advice on boards and other tips along the way, and it was a huge success, and most of the girls are regulars in the water to this day, which is great to see. Surfing has taken me all over the world, and now it feels like it's brought me home again.

COUNTERWORLD

RUSSELL CELYN JONES

SCENTS THAT BELONG TO THE WILD are appallingly sad when incarcerated, and when such a spoor her voice came spinning out, following him through the marina to where he had left his yacht. Now the only way to stop her voice carolling inside his head was to sail out to meet a storm in progress.

As he left the mainland behind, a great bank of violet cloud amassed in the sky. The wind hardened and his sails grew taut as skin over bone. As night fell it began to rain in sheets, blanketing the surface of the water. He brought the yacht down to storm canvas as seas lashed the deck and he heard the first crash of breaking crockery from below. On the crests he saw merchant ships running for cover. In the wave troughs he saw nothing at all. The going was claustrophobic and dark; the storm jib spilled the wind, the canvas flopped and mooned. Leaks appeared in the coach roof and between seals in the windows. His only home was structurally insecure. Yet the way she answered the lightest touch of the helm gave him pleasure. Through the darkness he saw the three white flashes every fifteen seconds of the Smalls Light, turning to red as he drifted into the explosives dumping ground off Hats and Barrels.

He was on the fringes of the storm now. A mile ahead the sea smoked blue and yellow. A tearing ebb tide meeting the wind carved huge escarpments in front of his eyes, waves that stood up on end like brick edifices. They slowed in speed but increased in height. The only light that could be had was from the phosphorescence on breaking crests and in their fiery wakes. The sea kept crashing onto his deck like something trying again and again to take possession. Sheets of water hitting him in the face, in the chest and knocking him down became routine. He was shivering inside his oilskins. Salt lined his mouth and burned his eyes.

This was as close as he could get to the point of no return. Sailing any further into the storm would be an act of self-destruction. He bore away with the boat hard down on its rail.

He'd gone ashore to buy a stern gland for the engine when he'd run into that scent escaping from a florist's door, reminding him so lethally of Laura and all the things she used to say. It had caught him off guard and then his heart began to ache.

They had met over twenty years ago at the age of thirty-three, and so confident of their love they wanted the world to know. But the world then was in bad shape, at least through their eyes. With an innocence it staggers him to think of now, they believed the world would improve if only it could be infected by their love. Everywhere they looked they saw the machinations of a police state, a repressive anti-working-class establishment. Out of love they shared a great indignation and held out the prospect of a better world that would be worthy of them. It took them a little while to find the right party to join, whose members talked in similar utopian undertones about fashioning a new future. Followers of Trotsky, this party had cadres all over the country, in industry, universities and unions. And as soon as they became active within its ranks, Travis and Laura discovered it was also an entrist organisation, infiltrating the Labour Party from top to bottom, from the National Executive to the Young Socialists. But by then it was too late to reassess their commitment to the revolution. They knew too much for the party ever to consider releasing them. In time, the party became a sort of family without children, and the secrecy of the movement added to their sense of cohesion. Its siege-like mentality enfranchised them.

For ten years they kept their faith, kept on course for a more just future, in which military generals, admirals, senior civil servants, police chiefs, judges would be sacked and the systems they once represented replaced by a socialist state. There would be an end to unemployment, wasteful advertising, the monarchy, the House of Lords. Science and medicine would reach their full potential and eradicate illness, pollution, poverty and wars. Capitalism was on the brink of collapse, or so they believed. They waited for Britain to teeter on the verge of social anarchy and then their organisation would assume the leadership of the Labour Party and turn Britain into a socialist state.

But the revolution never happened. A new order did

evolve and it was the order of money. Currency is made from the wood of the primal forest and appeals to baser instincts than theirs. So they had squandered ten years of their lives on a lost cause. Something that started out of love now turned against that love and they began inflicting wounds on one another.

After sailing all day and through the night, he saw the low-lying Scilly Isles shimmering on the horizon. They didn't look solid forms at all and the separate islands split from the pack at the pace he approached, slowly gaining pigment and shape. Razorbills, gannets glided over the water in front of him. The wind had backed to the south-west by the time he got among the islands, on course for St Agnes. Soon he was struggling against the tide to keep two landmarks in transit so as not to collide with the Spanish Ledges, where he changed course again, sliding up past Cuckold's Ledge. He made his entry into Porth Conger between the Calf and Cow rocks, weaving through lobster-pot buoys and power-cable lines. With little more than a four-metre clearance, he motor-sailed onto a mooring, pulled up its rope on the hook and tied onto the bow cleat.

On such islands, where there is an absence of mechanical hectoring, the silence can itself be tangible. The air was pure and greening, cast by the hues of the ocean. This was where Laura lived. In all these years he'd known where to find her, but had avoided the place, like he avoided all memories of her, and now he was here he couldn't decide whether to go ashore or not.

Two fishermen in identical yellow oilskins were moving around near the quay; Siamese flames burning oxygen out of the air, their skin wrecked by the same sun, full heads of grey hair, several days' beard and impenetrable eyes. They didn't acknowledge his presence, declined even to look at him, and that further disorientated him, made him doubt his bearings. Maybe he'd slept without realising it, missed the Scillies completely and landed in the acoustically dead Zone of Silence off Vancouver Island, where no bells or sirens penetrate. He went below and brought his log up to date, an old routine that suddenly felt entirely pointless to him. It was obvious what he had to do. He changed out of oilskins and shaved in cold water, ate some water biscuits and cold baked beans. When he had nourished himself, made himself presentable, he lowered the tender off the side.

Bordering the path were fields of bright red and orange flowers. Garden walls vanished under cascading yellow blooms. Proteas pushed through outcrops of rocks. Out of this colour and bloom a woman appeared in the corner of his vision, pruning her wallflowers and dropping the foliage into a wheelbarrow. She was side on, her hair hiding her face. But as he closed in on her she disappeared inside her whitewashed cottage; a subtle but deliberate move by one person to avoid an encounter with a stranger, an island vicissitude. An after-image of her peach sweater and lemon ankle-length skirt remained.

The cottage door was ajar. Travis knocked gently, then stepped across the threshold, lowering his head to clear the door frame, and entered a small kitchen that was busy with earthenware pots stuffed with cut flowers. Shelves were stacked with dried herbs, cans of powdered milk, baked beans . . . the kind of supplies he kept on board. Carrots, beetroots and potatoes filled a wicker basket sitting on the flagstone floor. The scrubbed wooden table was buckled with deep grooves, and supported more flowers in vases.

The smell of flowers acted like a narcotic upon him. The mixed heavy scent of bridal-white trumpets, scarlet bells and orange daisies numbed him to her entrance. She emerged from the lounge and stood in the kitchen for several seconds before he could mumble an explanation. 'The door was open,' he said.

'I was just wondering whether I should believe my eyes.'

Her face was gently folded like water, the strong eyes surrounded by ripples of loose flesh. Her fair hair had acquired grey dusty streaks. She had the look of someone who has run from one thing and into something else she hadn't accounted for. Laura was a woman in the country, but the country was not in her. She was dressed in clothes that would be suitable to sleep in – an old Indian cotton shift and peach sweatshirt covering heavy breasts. He felt attracted immediately and checked it. Cradled in her arms was a large bunch of long-stemmed white narcissi.

'May I ask, is this pure coincidence?'

Travis smiled awkwardly but said nothing. She didn't smile at all. The space between them was as much a work of the imagination to fill as of memory.

The platitudes continued a while, which neither he nor Laura would be able to recall. So overwhelmed nothing they said could stick. Words flying out of their mouths dispersed like smoke. That they'd once had a relationship that began over twenty years ago seemed more like an unconfirmed rumour. Their former intimacy was on a shelf too high to reach. The only agreement they could make was to take a walk outside.

Strolling in the direction of the disused lighthouse she asked, 'How did you get here? The ferry's not running yet.' He heard the torn fabric of her voice.

'I sailed.'

'You have a yacht?'

'In Porth Conger.'

'If the wind changes you're going to have to move it. To Killier or Periglis.'

'Depends on how long I stay.'

'What does that depend on?'

Travis didn't reply, didn't know how to reply. That decision was too far in the future. He continued looking at her, through her. He had to play this one out for as long as it felt right to do so. The silence stretched between them, matched by the silence around them.

He tried to imagine her living on this salt-blasted rock, sleeping through its harsh winters in a cell of a cottage. If she'd transformed the emptiness he felt there into an elevated state of being, he couldn't tell by looking at her. He didn't know who she was any more. The former political activist had become something other. Yet he was keen to discover her secret for combating emptiness. It might help him combat his own. But such questions were beyond his ability to compose. To understand her, her emotions, even her morality, he was just going to have to read the stones, the gorse and the flowers in this Zen garden in the sea.

Near the western reach of the island, she showed off the field where she grew various breeds of narcissi. Most of the flowers had been harvested, yet he could still smell a powerful scent from the path. The bi-coloured Soleil D'Or was her main crop. Other blooms included the Scilly White, obtained by the monks of St Nicholas from France and the Grand Monarch, which came from China. There were Primo, Avalance, King Alfred and Fortune trumpets growing in the field, surrounded with escallonia hedges as a windbreak. She explained how she parboiled the bulbs in warm water to accelerate growth, with a dash of formalin to destroy eel-worm, and heated the soil with propane gas.

It was aversion-talk and they both knew it.

A whole orchestra was playing in the sky. It was the migratory season and different species of birds were singing their regrets. She said how every night for the past two weeks birds had been fluttering around the lighthouse on Bishop's Rock, creating a blizzard effect in the rotating beams. In the morning hundreds of dead birds that had flown too hard at the light lay at the base of the lighthouse.

Now he did ask her what it was like to live on a tiny island, what isolation felt like to her. 'I have friends . . . farmers and fishermen and their wives. I know people on Tresco and on Bryher. Not so many from St Mary's. They're all Tories there.' She darted him a sly look that connected to the past.

The wind was still pouring in from the south-west, fresh and stiffening. He kept one eye on the clouds forming over Fastnet and the other on the coastal path along which they progressed in single file. Walking behind him, she pulled on his sleeve as they passed a chambered entrance under a granite slab. 'They found a skeleton inside there a few years ago, sitting up and begging. Some old hero who came here to die. Did you know King Arthur's buried in the Scillies?'

'Arthur's got about six hundred burial sites,' he said.

'Everyone tries to claim him as theirs, but only Scilly has the real man.'

He was wondering how a dialectical materialist becomes a mythologist, when she continued: 'Some of the outlying islands were inhabited by women only. Imagine that, Travis.'

'Maybe they lured Arthur onto the rocks.'

By now they were sitting on a bench. He wondered if she'd come here to die, too, along with all the holy men and heroes who'd hoped to find immortality in a mild climate. Certainly there was a feel of death all around, emanating from the Western Rocks that pierced the sea like rows of broken teeth. They too were burial grounds, but for men who'd not chosen to die. For African slaves who'd not even chosen to sail. Ten thousand men were incarcerated out there – two thousand from the same naval fleet of Sir Cloudesley Shovel, who escaped the wreck of his flagship with his treasure chest and pet greyhound until an island woman found him and slit his throat for his emerald ring.

This was a lethal place Travis had sailed into. 'You have a fearsome reputation,' he said after they'd been silent some minutes. 'I felt a little nervous coming in.'

She broke into his thoughts faster than he could form a defence. 'The Vikings came here for the tin. The Romans used it as a penal colony. The Spanish eyed up the place as a launching pad for their English offensive. No man comes here just for fun. So why have you come, Travis?'

He turned away from her to the spinal Western Rocks, an image for the end of all journeys. He had no answers to give about lost futures, lost love, and wandered away from her down the path to where the sea stirred like a hunchback in its sleep, shifting around its underwater freight. It moaned, gurgled and sighed. The sea that produced all sorts of noises, including the sound of asphyxia, was now the foundation for his own nomadic life, with limpets, crabs, snails and bloodsuckers as his neighbours. It was a single mass of mindless energy, a shifting desert, a killing floor.

She caught up with him on the path where he was standing staring out to sea. 'I think I'm going mad,' he said.

Laura started to laugh, covering her mouth with her hand and spilling apologies through her cracked fingers. It wasn't funny, but he laughed anyway, despite himself, his seriousness, and it brought him momentarily back to life. With that sensation came a stirring of a historic sexual attraction.

They walked back past the primary school Margaret

Thatcher had visited near the end of her reign, after being betrayed by her cabinet on her return from a Paris summit. They'd asked her to resign and she came out here. 'Of course, the old girl chose to come on Saturday, when the school was closed,' Laura said. 'The kids turned out anyway and watched the Grand National with her on TV. She was charmed, apparently. It is quite idyllic, I suppose. Children walk to school and pick wild flowers on the way home. No cars, no perverts hiding in bushes.'

Every year Laura went to the mainland before harvesting began in October; every moment she spent on the mainland was a moment lost, she said. On this point Travis agreed; the rituals of mainland Britain were alien to him, too. The car-infested towns, the monotonous suburbs, the constant catcalls about where to go, what to do when you get there, what to wear.

'That's why I live on an island too, all boats are islands.'

'Our ancestors built temples to their gods,' she said, 'and we build shopping malls. Don't tell me the world's progressed.'

'There was a time when we wanted to progress it . . . by force.'

She wasn't drawn by the personal code in this statement and said instead how baffling it was that the British had prevailed against organised Marxist-Leninist movements while allowing themselves to be colonised in the Tory southern heartlands by hordes of Eastern European refugees, many from USSR satellite nations.

He wanted to know, outright, whether she'd changed her political views.

'I haven't changed my views. They've just evolved. This life I lead is the alternative collective life we were seeking. The only change I've made is realising you can't force everyone to live this way. That was a great arrogance.' She smiled at him for an unnaturally long time. 'And I realised you can't live in the future indefinitely. Birds don't live in the future. Fish don't live in the future. But we tried to, for too long, and then disappeared.'

While they'd been tramping around the island he'd noticed several people keeping vigil on them through binoculars. 'What do you do here for fun? Apart from spying on one another?'

She slipped her hand inside his arm and he felt the warmth of her wrist burning his own. 'I don't know what you mean by fun. I work to eat, eat to work. What greater pleasure is there than that?'

He told her the only work he'd been engaged with, off and on, for the past eleven years was at an oceanography centre, using satellite technology to scan the oceans for severe weather conditions and trying to link it to climate change.

They returned to her cottage to sit in her garden as the last of the daylight receded over the island. Her garden was a map of flowers. Biting stonecrop, a star-shaped yellow flower, draped over her walls like rugs. Around the edges of her lawn were Hottentot fig – a South African iceplant with magenta flowers that could survive gale-force winds and driving salt spray. There were red campion, clusters of pink oxalis from South America, Mediterranean bear's breeches, whistling Jacks – like scarlet bells on stalks – and arum lilies. As windbreaks she'd planted veronica from New Zealand and a few stiff Monterey pines from California. Surrounding the garden table were tree echiums, a strange semi-tropical plant eight feet high with purple flowers in dreadlocks.

They drank tea with powdered milk and ate freshly baked soda bread with peanut butter. The way she poured him tea reminded Travis of something else. 'I can never forget how the comrades made you make the tea in our weekly meetings.'

'The comrades were very unenlightened in many ways.'

And with that they suddenly dropped right back into the centre of things. But it wasn't their vision of a counterworld they remembered, it was the fateful decision they made to postpone a family. It was more a pact than a decision. But in any case the revolution had cost them a family. There were no children in either of their lives and he felt it keenly now, marked by another period of stony silence.

They sat in her garden as the last of the light slanted across the earth and darkness began to fall over the island. An audible shrieking drifting from off the coast alarmed Travis. She explained that it was shearwaters reuniting with their life-long and monogamous partners in the nest as they returned from feeding binges in the Atlantic. Then she asked if he wanted to stay. As a matter of protocol she offered him the sofa, but was kidding no one. Sleeping with a person again after an eleven-year lapse can be the closest you get to living in history. But if she wanted to feel how his body had aged, he felt the distance still. The leap from talking to sleeping together was too big.

Finally he said, 'I should go to my yacht. If the wind changes I'm going to have to move it.'

Early next morning he was sitting in the cockpit, meditating on the jagged Western Rocks when Laura rowed out. She carried a large bouquet of white narcissi on the thwart as though on her way to a Viking funeral.

'You came to visit me in my house,' she shouted over the wind, 'I thought I'd come visit you in yours.'

He leaned over the side and took her rope, tying it on to a stern cleat. He relieved her of the flowers as she landed clumsily inside the cockpit with the wind blowing her hair into her face. They sat side by side as the yacht rocked gently in the calm water and as he rocked back and forth with his chin low on his chest. In his arms he cradled the flowers.

'Actually I was afraid you'd take off this morning without saying goodbye.'

'I'm only waiting to leave with the tide.'

She put her arm around him and brushed her fingers across his forehead, recalling other times when she'd offered solicitude. But she didn't understand him any more, didn't know what to tell him. Men's despair is only truly understood by other men. All she could say was, 'Why not stay on for a few days?' When he didn't answer she added, 'You can't live on a boat for ever, Travis.'

'I don't see why not.'

'When men go travelling they are left with only themselves.'

'You are left with only yourself.'

'I still have my feelings for you. You don't always have to
be in the presence of the object for love to be revelatory.'

What was she saying? What she was saying was nothing. He was all at sea with her words, could feel the current
of time pulling him under. His mouth grew bone dry and
he was finding it harder to breathe. Cold sweat broke out
on his chest and on his palms. He began to fear he would
break into tiny fragments and be scattered over the sea.

Before he left he invited her to go with him. It was a
gesture neither one believed. She could no more accept
his offer to share his home than he could accept hers. 'My
love for you may be resilient, Travis, but can't survive
seasickness.'

She slipped off the side into her small boat. He watched
her row to shore, then left St Agnes on the engine, following the pilotage instructions to clear the underwater cables,
channels and sandbars into St Mary's Sound. When the
north corner of Mincario and Great Minalto islands came
in line, he altered course to 053 and glided over the sub-
marine exercise area.

He rounded Wolf Rock just as the tide changed direction in his favour, pushing him along to Lizard Point. By
force of habit he maximised his boat's efficiency even without a destination, reducing leeway and trimming the sails
constantly as the wind strengthened. He engaged the
Autohelm and radar alarm and dissolved into the big sky,

into tiny parcels of sleep. He was still on this eastern tack several hours later when he suddenly changed his mind, changed course for the west.

For another four hours he maintained a reach. A beam reach is a pleasant sailing position. Great pleasure comes from balancing the main and genoa, in hearing the sails inhale the wind. Then Scilly appeared again off the starboard quarter. The enchantment of the islands was irresistible but he fought it off anyway, altering course again to close haul up the north-west wind, making for the southern tip of Ireland.

The weather near the Irish coast held fine. There was a gold sheen to the sea. But after leaving Cape Clear behind he started to feel the swell running under the yacht. He picked up a storm warning from the coastal radio station at Baltimore and headed in that direction. A force-ten storm was two hours away.

Of the two thousand storms in progress at sea at any given moment, no two are the same. Some have multiple centres of depression; some are thunder and lightning induced. None are house-trained. They pay the most unexpected visits. Some stay four hours while others take twenty-four hours to blow out. He had no idea what this one would be like when he got there. Its character would be all its own.

After he had sailed for two more hours, the waves had reached their maximum height over a thirty-mile fetch, a composition of swells outside their area of generation and surface waves in perpetual conference. Travis studied them fiercely from the cockpit, tying to take his mind off her and return to himself. Where the swell and surface waves met the strength and height of the combined waves was the addition of each for a few seconds, before splitting apart and going in different directions, diminished in size once again. Every eight to ten minutes, two swells in a train got into step, and he noticed the seventh and eleventh swell in sequence were always the highest of the group. Every twenty-third swell was twice the height of the average. This is how freak waves occur, when a wave travelling fastest in its group picks up other waves, confiscating their energy and strength. A freak wave has a short life and can expire just as quickly as a wave a third its size. But if you are in the way at its moment of greatest strength then the odds are against you. Odds like 1 in 23 (twice the average height); 1 in 1175 (three times the average height). He was surrounded by prime, rational numbers and he was in chaos.

He was thirty miles out in the Atlantic, fighting the big seas. His Decca was letting him down. Its signals were getting weaker the further he sailed into the storm. His GPS handset was giving him a reading but he didn't believe that either. His yacht was under solid water almost permanently. In a force-ten storm everything becomes a battle to keep the yacht afloat. The force of this storm was stunning and bold. He didn't know for how much longer she could hold up. Eventually he sheeted in the storm jib and lashed the tiller, locking the boat in the water. An hour before, his yacht had been a thing of life. Now it was a dead weight hanging in the sea.

Going below he found in the saloon a shambles of flung crockery and pots, like the forlorn aftermath of some marital brawl. Water in the bilges had risen to above the sole. It leaked through window seals, cracks edging the cockpit lockers, the ventilation and the cabin hatch. He lay in his settee berth and in the close, damp atmosphere watched the leaks and the condensation running down the bulkheads. Not for a second did the yacht stop shaking and trembling, nor did the noise of the sea abate. He monitored transmissions on the radio, the lonely sound of masters' voices in Russian; his unknown neighbours in an unknown place talking to one another, bridge to bridge, with the intimacy of spouses. In that same moment something became finally clear to him. The future was already existing, as surely as the past, and had been merely awaiting his arrival. He had reached the future and there was nothing to do now but survive it the best he could.

THE WISDOM OF THE
LIGHTHOUSE KEEPERS

PETER HILL

JUST AS THE WORLD IS coming to appreciate the philosophy of 'slow' – slow living, slow cities, slow cooking – lighthouse keepers, the real champions of *slow*, have been made totally redundant. But their wisdom lives on.

One of the happiest summers of my life was in 1973 when I worked as a relief lighthouse keeper on three uninhabited islands off the west coast of Scotland. Uninhabited, that is, except for the glorious, warm and eccentric company of around a dozen fine men with whom I worked on the islands of Pladda, Ailsa Craig and Hyskeir. Collectively, they taught me a great deal. It was as if I had entered a great learning machine, as complex as the routine of keeping the light itself. Green around the gills, I went into the machine a twenty-year-old hippie art student with my Captain Beefheart tapes, my Jack Kerouac novels, my frayed jeans and my hand-rolling tobacco, and I emerged six months later able to cook, fish, polish brass until it shone like butter, stay awake through the wee small hours and, most important, keep the light burning and turning. But my real education came at the change of watch, especially at two in the morning, when stories would be told to help the keeper coming on duty stay awake and alert for the long, dark hours ahead. This was when I learned that Vietnam was not the only war that had been fought for all the wrong reasons, that Nixon and Kissinger not the only corrupt politicians, and that the old men with whom I worked (or so they seemed to this child of the 1960s) had been young once themselves. Probably the greatest thing they taught me was how it is possible to work together, even if you have differences, and that an ounce of good humour is worth a ton of bossiness or bullying. Your life may one day depend on your fellow keepers, and theirs on you – it doesn't get much simpler than that. And while there are no churches, universities or government buildings on lighthouse islands, there is a great deal of wisdom to be found amongst the men who work there.

Importantly, each keeper had his very own individual take on life. Most had lived adventurous lives in the merchant navy, as firemen in big cities, as gold prospectors in Australia, or submariners in the Second World War. For them, becoming lighthouse keepers had been a sea change, almost like retiring into a new kind of life. It was the sort of thing cashed-up city stock traders do today, but much more fun. And the tips on life that each of them gave me at two in the morning – Finlay Watchorn, Duncan, Ronnie, Stretch and the Professor – I now refer to as the Wisdom of the Lighthouse Keepers. And you know, I think the world would be a far safer place today if it was run by lighthouse keepers instead of politicians. It would certainly be more relaxed. Drop a few Iraqi, American, French,

North Korean, British and Australian lighthouse keepers
on an uninhabited island for a long weekend and they'd
have it all sorted out by Monday – probably over a large pot
of tea and an endless supply of biscuits and cheese. Saving
lives, of course, is their whole reason for being. But sadly
there are no lighthouse keepers left any more.

Thirty years later, when I was about to turn fifty and now
living on the other side of this infuriatingly wonderful
planet, I decided to set off and visit some of the lighthouses
that shine like an ocean necklace around the enormous
coastlines of Australia and New Zealand. I packed my
Pogues tapes – good for take-offs and landings – some
Albinoni for quieter periods, a copy of Robert Louis
Stevenson's *Travels with a Donkey*, and the latest edition of
the *New Yorker*. I also took an old copy of the *Lighthouse
Journal* (Summer 1989), as I do on all my travels. It is, or
was, the magazine sent out by my former paymasters, the
grandly named Commissioners of the Northern Lights –
all of whom were usually tucked up in bed well before midnight in their Georgian houses in Edinburgh's New Town.
But most importantly, at the back of my mind, I unpacked
my memories that I'd kept all these years. I'd take them
with me and see how useful they'd be in the early years of
the twenty-first century.

The first piece of wisdom that I wanted to put to the test
was Finlay Watchorn's oft-made claim that the shorter a
period of time you spent in any one place the more you
remembered about it. He learned this during his time in

the Merchant Navy, where he had also picked up his gourmet cooking skills. I remember that the first time he told me about this, he was making a lamb kebab with some meat that had been defrosting overnight. 'Think about it,' he said. 'If you spend six months in a place, doesn't matter whether it's a big port like Rotterdam or a small harbour town like Stromness, it all becomes very familiar. But if you're only there twenty-four hours you keep getting lost – especially after a few nippy sweeties. All things are new, the language and accents are different, strange smells fill the air, you remember where you've just come from and where you are headed, and because of all this it really stamps itself on your memory. And that's just on this side of our dear little planet. Down in South America, or Australia, or South Africa, suddenly it's summer when it should be winter and everything is topsy-turvy. I once had Hogmanay and New Year's Day in Sydney before we sailed for Wellington. God it was amazing, down on the beach, blue skies, beautiful women, light until ten at night. Me and the lads got a wee poker school going under this palm tree. I think the place was called Manly, something like that. But dinnae tell Duncan about the cards and the girls or he'll start going on about fornicators and the Devil's pictures.' Duncan was the elderly PLK (Principal Lighthouse Keeper) on Pladda, and a staunch member of the Wee Free Church, for whom today's *slow* movement might seem a bit too exciting.

This whole adventure would, on and off, take over two years to complete and cover a distance equal to the cir-

cumference of the planet. My first target was to get to Cape
Leveque lighthouse in a remote Aboriginal community
north of Broome. Australia is the world's largest island and
roughly the size of the USA. I once found a wall clock, in a
garage sale, made in the shape of Australia. It was so kitsch
that I had to buy it. Sydney, where I lived when this adventure began, is roughly at 5 p.m. on the face of the clock, its
beautiful harbour, with Opera House and bridge, spilling in
to the South Pacific. Diagonally across – way, way across, as
Dublin is way, way across from Teheran – at 10 p.m. on the
dial, lies Broome on the warm waters of the Indian Ocean.
Right in the centre where the hands of the clock join is
Uluru, or Ayers Rock as it was formerly known, the world's
strangest monolith. It is roughly the same height as Ailsa
Craig, where my second lighthouse was situated, midway
between Glasgow and Belfast. Far to its north, at midnight
on the clock, is the city of Darwin. I mention all this because
in order to afford to get from Sydney to Broome and still be
able to afford accommodation, I'd have to use frequent flyer
points. I gave the good people at Qantas a bell.

'Sorry, sir,' Trudy the call-centre hostess told me from a
cubicle somewhere in Brisbane, Hobart, or possibly New
Delhi. 'I can't get you a return from Sydney to Broome on
points until a couple of weeks after the school holidays. Let
me have a look and see if there are any alternative routes.'
The wait was long, but in the end, worth it. I groaned
through almost three minutes of a trad-jazz version of Lou
Reed's 'Satellite Of Love' before Trudy rescued me with the
following offer.

'What I can do is a single from Sydney to Alice Springs.' The red heart of the continent, not far from Uluru – I was intrigued. 'Then if you are happy to wait for a couple of hours, there's a flight up to Darwin I can get you on, but you'll have to stay overnight.' Darwin! The only capital city in Australia I'd still to visit. Barrie Magic, as they say in Edinburgh. I was beginning to like the sound of this. 'Then next day afternoon I can get you on a flight to Broome and return you direct to Sydney three days later.' It was a done deal, one that Tony Soprano would have been proud of. Just before hanging up I asked Trudy if she had some charts that could work out how long the round-trip would be. With barely a pause she said, 'It's about nine thousand and six hundred kilometres. Half your luck.' Half a continent, I thought, speechless, as all my frequent flyer points flew out the window.

Before leaving Sydney I found myself a second-hand copy of *The Short Stay Guide to the Northern Territory*. Not until I was firmly strapped into my seat for the flight out of Alice Springs across the northern half of the continent did I turn to the index and locate Darwin. I read with heightened anticipation that: 'Through the decades, Darwin town gained a reputation as a frontier of prawn trawlers, buffalo catchers, croc shooters and wild waterfront bars. It was the boozing capital of a thirsty nation.' Sounded like my kinda toon, I thought. The writer of these words, Chris Baker, sketched in more of the background history to the place, as my eyes darted eagerly between the red desert below the plane and the white pages of text leaning on the fold-down tray in front of me. 'Records show the first European explorers arrived in 1623 aboard the Dutch ship, *Arnhem* . . . Darwin harbour was discovered in 1839 by the first officer of the HMS *Beagle*, and was named in honour of Charles Darwin, who had sailed on an earlier expedition on the ship. It was a strategic outpost for the British during the Second World War, and suffered tremendous damage during 64 air raids, with the loss of 243 lives. The Tiwi people on Bathurst Island, who were the first to see the Japanese bombers, perform a corroboree (dance) that tells the story.'

About the only other thing I knew about Darwin was that it had been hit by a humungous cyclone – Cyclone Tracy – on Christmas Eve in 1974. Chris Baker describes it as 'one of the greatest natural disasters in Australian history', and reports that it 'left only about 500 of the city's then 8000 homes habitable. Today Darwin is considered a relaxed tropical city with a relatively young population numbering above 70,000.'

I was going to have less than twenty-four hours here, and planned to hit the tarmac running.

Although my time in Darwin would be brief, and an ideal test of Finlay Watchorn's words of wisdom, I realised in the taxi driving into the city that I was under absolutely no pressure. As we drove past Fannie Bay Gaol and along palm-tree-lined freeways under the domed blue sky, I realised I had no meetings to go to, no journalistic deadlines to meet for a few days, no appointments with friends, or family commitments.

'Would you mind just driving around the town a bit?' I asked the driver, deciding to take full advantage of the situation. 'I've never been here before and wouldn't mind getting my bearings.' The taxi looked like it had just rolled off the Mercedes Benz production line. It had that new-car smell with matching pride of ownership. The friendly young Chinese driver, wearing a white short-sleeved shirt and heavy gold watch, explained that he did mostly corporate work for the big Asian companies who took advantage of Darwin's tax breaks on raw materials.

I was enjoying the thrill of excitement that comes with new road signs pointing to exotic-sounding places – Humpty Doo, Rum Jungle, Darwin Crocodile Farm, Melacca Swamp – which might, given the size of the Northern Territory, be a thousand miles away or just around the corner. The Northern Territory occupies over one-sixth of Australia's great landmass, yet has less than 150,000 people, half of whom live in Darwin. Mind-boggling!

Charlie, as he introduced himself, pointed out the Diamond Beach Casino and hinted that he had more than a passing familiarity with its games of crap, blackjack and two-up. I'd expected a lot of new buildings and standardised housing after the ravages of Cyclone Tracy. What I hadn't expected was the lush greenery, which didn't stop at the city's outskirts but accompanied us in. Sometimes it expanded into parks, or squeezed itself along hibiscus-dripping nature strips. Sometimes it rolled towards the sea, then doubled back into town. The wet season must be pretty wet, I thought, for the dry season to be so green. And framing this tropical greenness was the white of concrete buildings that stood squatly to attention.

'We call these buildings "six-packs",' Charlie told me. 'They're all post-cyclone, of course. Built very quickly. There's an interesting nature walk just down there. It takes you to a place called Doctor's Gully where you can hand-feed fish – thousands of them, and big buggers too. Very colourful. It was a local doctor who started it in his retirement and it's become quite an attraction. You've got to be there at high tide though.'

'Tell me,' I asked, head still full of road signs. 'How does a place come to get called Humpty Doo?'

'You're not the first passenger to ask that, sir,' Charlie replied politely. 'There's always been a big Chinese community around Humpty Doo since early attempts at growing rice there. My great-great-grandparents were some of the first migrants there. They came north by coach and camel train after the Ballarat gold rush ended. On my mother's side of the family, you understand. As for the name, local lore says it was an early settler who used to travel into Darwin from there, and when asked how things were, his reply was, "Everything's Humpty Doo." And the name stuck.'

'Just down the road from Hunky Dory,' I added cheekily.

'Excuse me, sir?'

'Nothing, just a thought from afar . . . '

We cruised past the Esplanade and he pointed out my

hotel, which we would return to later. A quick circuit of Smith Street, Bennett, McMinn and Daly gave me the co-ordinates of the city grid, and I noted where the post office, newsagent's and Coles supermarket were situated. I'd visit them all later in the afternoon to procure refreshments and stamps.

Each end of the city leads down to either a wharf or a marina and we visited them both. We parked at the Stokes Hill Wharf and I got out to look at some of the shops and restaurants. They were all pretty much international bland, themed to look like a pale Rorschach blot of an original somewhere else on the planet. Similarly, the main drag up in the city had its Shennagins Irish Pub and its Rorke's Drift video bar. But each, no matter how themed, was pierced with local content that placed you precisely at the Top End, as this part of the continent is known. In a restaurant called Schnitzel Magic on the wharf, which I feared would be a culinary recreation of Old Vienna, I read on the chalkboard the specials of the day:

> Barramundi
> Crocodile
> Camel
> Squid
> Buffalo
> Kangaroo
> (All with Chips and Salad)

The bakery next door, which could have been modelled on

a Hansel and Gretel Gingerbread House, was offering a range of 'Pirate's Pies' with similarly exotic fillings for 'Meat Lovers', listed below a chalk-drawn skull and cross-bones.

From there we drove to the other side of the city, to Cullen Bay, which looked alarmingly like Sullivan's Cove in Hobart, Tasmania, which from here was several thousand kilometres towards the South Pole. Yachts bobbed in the marina, upmarket restaurants jostled against wine bars, and to my delight at the furthest arm-stretch of the bay we could just glimpse a lighthouse.

'That's Emery Point,' Charlie told me. 'But it's on an army reserve and we can't get access.' Bugger!

I checked up on it later, and it is – like many lights in the Top End – an open criss-cross construction of white girders with a beacon on the top. However, my main focus on this trip was to get to Cape Leveque lighthouse. But that was still three days and a couple of thousand kilometres away.

Up in my hotel room, after Charlie had finally dropped me off, I got out my maps and charts and had a proper squiz at the territory – the Northern Territory to be precise. About forty kilometres off the coast of Darwin are two islands – Bathurst and Melville – home of the Tiwi people. They are separated by a narrow strait, known as the Apsley Strait, which was missed by the early Dutch explorers in 1644. They thought it was a single island. For thousands of years the Tiwi people lived here, united by a common language and culture, unlike the Aborigines of mainland Australia. Cape Fourcroy sat at the far west of Bathurst Island, while out to the east were lights on Cape Don, Cape Crocker and New Year Island.

Beyond that is a mini-necklace of lighthouses that stretches many hundreds of kilometres from the Timor Sea, through the Arafura Sea and down into the Gulf of Carpenteria, where around Groote Eyelande there is a string of smaller lights and beacons. Plenty to come back to later, I assured Finlay Watchorn, who as ever was sitting on my left shoulder, egging me on. Another bit of his wisdom that I always remembered was that you should never try and exhaust a new destination on your first visit. 'Always keep a few things to do on your second visit, laddie. Did I ever tell you about my second trip to Morocco?'

I enjoyed my eighteen hours in Darwin. I spent most of my one evening there just strolling round the centre, looking at things, photographing signage, making notes and having the occasional cool beer after the fierce heat of the day. In one Wild West-style watering hole I met a crazy American called Drizzle who was writing a PhD on 'storm-chasers', always arriving a safe distance after the event. He bore an uncanny resemblance to James Joyce, with a black eye patch and a pair of heavy spectacles.

Elsewhere, I rather liked the way many inner-city hotels advertised 'Chilled Swimming Pool' as a selling point, and agreed with Finlay that had I stayed there a month I'd never have remembered it. The surprise factor would have vanished, along with my fascination for local menus and exotic street signs.

Most of the wildness in this 'wild frontier town' seemed to be coming from tourists who'd spent too long in the sun and then too long in the saloon, rather than the locals, who I found were all very friendly, laid-back and helpful.

Just before night fell – and it fell with tropical suddenness – I perused an open-fronted hut on the Esplanade, which told the story of Darwin's wartime bombing by the Japanese. 'Almost two hours after the first air raid, 54 land-based bombers attacked the Darwin RAAF Station. A total of 243 people died in the raids, eight ships sunk, many buildings were damaged, communications were cut and the township was shattered.'

These text displays with their sepia photographs hung on a green lattice grid through which I caught the fading sun on the dark-turning sea. I remembered once during a similarly brief sojourn in Hawaii on my way back to a Scottish Hogmanay, I'd gone out on a sailing ship with a boatload of mostly Japanese tourists to view Pearl Harbor. The tourism of war, the need for memorials, seemed to be as strong a force as cultural tourism, with its need for the sublime moment amidst the everyday. Port Arthur, Auschwitz, Culloden, Waterloo, Gallipoli . . . or would you rather go to Donald Judd's sculpture ranch at Marfa in Texas? I would. Perhaps Ian Hamilton Finlay's poetic Garden Temple, Little Sparta, on the Scottish moors south of Glasgow and Edinburgh, best combines the main elements of the sublime: a heightened consciousness of joy with the ever-present threat of terror.

My last two hours in Darwin were, in many ways, the best. I was travelling light, so on my way to the airport and my flight across the Top End to Broome, I took one taxi to the museum and art gallery, and would call another one later to complete the journey and catch my plane.

The great thing is that it was much more than an art gallery. First of all, it was set in lush botanic gardens. Banners outside advertised a Darwin contemporary art triennial, and a huge floating astronaut flagged a space exploration exhibit.

Time was short, so I didn't linger too long in the graphic Cyclone Tracy display, other than to marvel at the powers of nature on a bad day. Early Aboriginal paintings in the European watercolour tradition by several members of the same family were admirable but made me very happy that collectively the Aboriginal communities had followed the dotted path of its pioneers, Geoffrey Barden and Clifford Possum.

No, the big surprise for me was the huge extension at the back of the museum – think aircraft-hangar dimensions – which housed a comprehensive maritime museum. And it was a maritime museum that was not only flavoured by the Top End and its surrounding islands, it was *entirely* that.

To get into the extension, I had to pass a rather ferocious gatekeeper called Sweetheart, who ends up featuring in most travellers' accounts of Darwin. Sweetheart is an absolutely huge crocodile. If you are a two-car family and one of them is a four-wheel drive and the other a Volkswagen, imagine them parked bumper to bumper, and that is about the size of Sweetheart. I marvelled at the size of his teeth, and had been told his testicles were equally impressive. However, I wasn't convinced he was dead and safely stuffed – I knew these prehistoric beasts could be very patient – so there was no way I was going to have a squint at his nether regions. Before arriving here, I'd wondered whether the Northern Territory would downplay its crocs in case it scared away tourists, but having been to Far North Queensland – 'Beautiful One Day, Perfect the Next' as its tourism pitch goes – I was pretty sure they wouldn't. Around Darwin, as in Cairns, crocodiles featured on menus, in museums and as feeding events at special farms. Bizarrely, while Australia has no alligators, the Northern Territory has three rivers running through Kakadu reserve: West Alligator River, South Alligator River and East Alligator River. It turns out the Pom who named them was trained in surveying and not zoology. He'd probably have made a pretty meagre snack anyway. Sweetheart's claim to fame is that he did not attack people, but went ballistic when he heard the sound of motorboats. A lot of weekend sailors ended up very wet, but only their machinery was chewed to destruction. I edged past the enormous beast, alert for subdued breathing, and into the maritime wing.

The place was full of boats of all sizes, their sails erect

as if caught full breeze. The huge hangar – intersected with mezzanine walkways – was filled with light. The appealing aspect about the exhibits was that most of them had not been restored to their former glory but had been left sun-bleached and weathered. They all belonged to the general family of 'sailing craft' but they were all markedly different from each other. It reminded me of when I was a very young child and my father would show me the stacks upon stacks of boxes of insects in his study, towering high above the heavy black microscope and the formaldehyde specimen jars. Here was a box full of weevils, yet like these boats, they were all so different from each other, neatly pinned to tiny white squares of card like new shirts in a tailor's shop. Here was a box of moths, and another of butterflies, one as grey as porridge, the other rainbow-hued and glistening like an oil slick in the sun.

I could tell that one boat, its hull now faded, had once been painted like a fairground carousel with orchids and leaf fronds repeating and swirling round its hull and stern. But you had to look closely to discern the palimpsest that was the sun-cracked wooden hull, which could only be read like a skull beneath the skin.

Then there were the sails! The sails were all as different in colour, shape and texture as a walk round the Pompidou Centre's twentieth-century collection. Some were bold, like a Frank Stella, with a stripe of red on yellow. Others had a faded chequerboard effect in blues and greys with stripes of vermilion pink, like those Chinese bags you see at laundromats the world over, or at refugee checkpoints, stuffed with a lifetime's possessions. Probably made of the same material, I guessed.

Next to a glorious vessel that looked like a cross between a Viking longship and a candy-covered birthday cake, I read a text headed 'Bajau Lipa Lipa'. It began: 'The Bajau, or "sea gypsies" as they are often called, are a marvellous group of maritime people who have spread through much of Southeast Asia. Traditionally they lead a semi-nomadic life on the sea with each family using a house boat or *Lipa Lipa* as its home.'

A little further on, something low and sleek caught my eye. It had the sort of design lines that made you think 'shark' or 'torpedo', but it was definitely a boat. In fact, it was a Vietnamese refugee boat with the rather pretty name of *Thinh Voong*, which the label told me meant 'prosperity'.

'It arrived in Darwin in June 1978 with 9 people on board,' I read, fascinated that there was a real human story attached to the craft in front of me and it hadn't just been 'bought in' as an example, or specimen. 'Following the end of the American-Vietnam war, thousands of refugees fled their homeland in fishing boats and other small vessels.'

But astonishment was to build on astonishment as I came next upon a huge dugout canoe from Tanimbar Island in Indonesia. At the height of the cyclone season it had drifted across the Arafura Sea while attempting to make the very short trip across the Ergon Straits from one little island to an even smaller one – and I thought of Arran to Pladda thirty years ago. Their 'drift', as such a journey is called, took the four men, two women and four children 333km (180 miles) towards the Top End of Australia, where they were picked up just off the Cape Don lighthouse and taken to Darwin. During the long voyage they had survived on a little corn, some dried fish and rainwater. 'It is unusual to find such a large, well-made canoe with no "strakes" (planks) to increase its freeboard and sea-keeping ability.'

But it was what came next that for me was like finding a nugget of gold just lying at my feet. I should tell you that there are two artists – one Australian, one Scottish – whose lives have become fascinating for me because of their extraordinary adventurous quality and their love of islands and adventures. One is John Peter Russell, the Australian Impressionist, who befriended Van Gogh and Toulouse Lautrec, married Rodin's model, went to live in a huge house on the Belle Isle off the Brittany coast, and painted there with both Monet and, later, Matisse.

In Hilary Spurling's gripping biography *The Unknown Matisse*, the one-time literary editor of the *Spectator* writes: 'Matisse himself said that it was Russell who introduced him to the Impressionists' theories of light and colour, in particular to the innovations of Claude Monet, setting technical exercises to help him assimilate them in practice.' Shortly before Rodin died, in his last letter to Russell he said, 'Your works will live, I am certain. One day you will be placed on the same level with our friends Monet, Renoir and Van Gogh.'

By contrast to the born-into-wealth Russell, the Scottish

artist Ian Fairweather turned his back on money, instead courting poverty and the freedom it gave him. Born near Crieff in Scotland, he was educated by aunts in London, attended the Slade and ended up travelling widely in China, studying calligraphy, and ending his days on Bribie Island off the Queensland coast of Australia. Most of his paintings, which were like an independent flourishing of Abstract Expressionism – particularly pre-drip-and-dribble Jackson Pollock – were made on cardboard,[1] hence they haven't travelled and he is barely known at all outside Australia. He should be in every twentieth-century art book, in my opinion. I'd heard vague stories that he'd made a dangerous raft journey at one point in his life, and this is the point at which I stumbled on my nugget of gold. On the wall-text that described the journey of the six-metre dugout canoe that sat before me, I read the concluding paragraph. 'Since 1950 only two small drift craft have gone in the opposite direction. One was that of artist Ian Fairweather, who launched his raft from the Fannie Bay foreshore near to where the Museum and Art Gallery of the Northern Territory stands today.' Perhaps, I thought, one day I will write a book about artists who lived on islands. And Fairweather and Russell will be top of my list.

---

[1] His Sydney gallery would keep sending him big rolls of canvas, only to receive friendly replies along the lines of: 'Thanks for the canvas. I've made a new tent and some trousers.' And he would continue happily painting on the sides of cardboard boxes.

I savoured the image of Fairweather pushing off in his little craft from the very spot where I was standing, now waiting for a taxi to rush me to the airport for my flight across desert, ocean and mangrove forest, to Broome on the high shoulder of the Indian Ocean. I'd enjoyed Darwin. 'Not bad,' I remarked to Finlay, perched on my shoulder, 'for eighteen hours. I'll definitely be coming back for second helpings.'

THREE WOMEN, AND
SOMETHING ELSE

ERICA WAGNER

'You can't stay,' Xanthe said.

'I can,' he said. 'I asked.' The clerk at the desk had seen Xanthe loading the car, but Dan had said: 'I'll keep the room.' The fellow – who was also the barman at night – had shrugged. Of course. It was winter. He could keep the room for as long as he liked, now the weekend was over.

'That's not what I mean.' She was standing over him, her hands flat on the yellow cloth on the table. 'You know that's not what I mean.' Their car was parked outside, ready to go. It was Sunday. The December sunshine was brittle and knife-bright on the promenade, on the freezing sea; in the boot of the car was the bounty they'd bought in their effortful festivity: wine, crème de pêche, cheese, salty caramels.

He didn't answer her. Last night, in the hotel's restaurant, à Montrachet, goose liver hot with fat on a white plate, the other diners, mostly English, laughing and toasting each other with the generous bowls of their glasses. Dan in his suit, Xanthe in the red skirt he'd bought her from Agnès B, the bleached haze of her hair pulled back with a velvet tie, the dark roots of it framing her face. But then, later, in the warm hotel dark behind the curtains, her hands on his chest, on his neck, and his silence and stillness. He heard her crying. He didn't move. He wanted to. He could not.

'You take the car,' he said finally. 'I'll get a taxi. Tomorrow. To – Fréthun, isn't it? I'll just get on the train to Waterloo.'

'You really want to stay here by yourself.' A statement.

'I don't have any teaching until Wednesday.'

'You won't come back until Wednesday?'

'I didn't say that. I said I had to teach Wednesday, in any case. I'd have to be back by then.'

'I'm not a child, Dan; don't talk to me like I am one.'

He knew the face she was wearing, knew it so well, her sharp chin set out, her unwillingness to be hurt, her wish to protect herself. He had wished to protect her too, but he had not succeeded. 'I know that,' Dan said. 'I know.' Outside on the promenade a man rollerbladed by, his legs swinging, his arms locked behind his back, earphones clamped to the sides of his head. The sea called out, and called again. The water moved like cloth, tearing and mending, tearing and mending. A jetty stretched out into the tide. For a moment something beyond the jetty caught his eye. Not a boat. Smaller than that, but not a bird either. His breath seized briefly; as if he were in a car and he would need to hit the brakes. Then it was gone, the feeling, whatever it was that had been in the water.

'Dan,' she said. 'Dan.' She was dry-eyed now. Her black fleece made her face look pale and tired.

'You could stay,' he said.

'You don't mean that.'

He didn't have an answer.

'What will you do?' she asked. She sat down, then, across from him, as if they were friends.

'I don't know,' he said. 'I thought I might go to Arras. Or Agincourt. We never got there.'

'So you'll go on your own.'

He nodded.

'How will you get there? Without the car.'

'There must be buses,' he said. 'Or something.'

Everyone else had gone from the breakfast lounge. Xanthe looked down at the table, then out to the water. He did the same.

'I'll be home tomorrow,' he said again. 'Or Tuesday. I'll call you.' He picked up a tiny spoon, set it down again with a click in the saucer of his cup.

'Well,' she said eventually. 'I'll finish packing.' When she'd gone he poured the dregs of the coffee from the jug. It was cold. He could have asked for more. He did not.

There had been a show, a gallery in Mayfair. Every few months the place turned itself over to students; Xanthe knew one of the art teachers who'd swung the deal. They'd met there after work – Dan from the university where he was just about to be made a full professor, Xanthe from the studio where she worked as a producer. It was March, cool and rainy. Afterwards he always remembered the rain; or, hardly rain at all but a steady mist hanging in the air, blurring the street lights and laying slicks of glare along the pavement under his feet.

He didn't like what he saw. The wine was bad, warm and greeny, and the gallery was full of people with crooked hair. There were sculptures made of wire, plastic and tampons; there was an empty glass case with a label beneath it copied from the Pitt-Rivers Museum. Dan was hungry, and he wanted to leave almost immediately. He had lost Xanthe, her small form sucked into the jittery crowd. Scanning the room for her, he liked the little edge of discomfort he felt – a reminder of their differences. He could laugh at himself – he felt young to be here, with Xanthe's people, although they weren't really; but they were, like Xanthe, mostly younger than he was, at the beginning rather than somehow in the middle. Sometimes Xanthe teased him, called him *my old man* although there were only nine years between them. He had an image of his hands on Xanthe's waist; of her sitting on the side of the bath, a towel around her head, the smell of bleach. Then he looked at his watch. He really was hungry. They could go out to eat. He pushed himself through the crowd, to where he saw Xanthe standing near the rear of the gallery, talking to a tall man in a bright green suit. He bent down to her.

'Come on,' he said. 'I'm starving.'

'Just wait,' she said, and abandoned the green suit, pulling Dan down to her, a stage whisper at his cheek. 'It's awful, isn't it? All of it. Except . . . ' and she tugged at his sleeve, dragging them both through the crowds and towards the back wall, where three dark paintings hung.

Rothko? Dan thought, though he didn't know quite where that came from; but no, these weren't like those louring slabs of colour. You'd have to call these figurative, though it would be hard to say what the figures were. The figures, however, seemed certain enough of themselves.

'These are Claire's,' Xanthe said. 'Oh, and look – Claire!' Xanthe called out. Claire turned towards them both, and smiled.

He didn't go to Agincourt. For a long time he sat, his cold coffee in front of him. The clerk helped the two waitresses clear away the detritus from breakfast. The three of them were neat and brisk: the man in pressed black trousers and a bright crisp shirt, white with a candy-green stripe; the women, one blonde, one dark, in short but not too short black skirts and blue shirts with white collars. The blonde came up to clear his table, smiled at him apologetically, and he nodded and pushed his chair back, allowing her to take away the coffee cups, the jug, the white plates with their smears of butter and crumbs.

Outside the plate-glass windows the promenade was filling up. Though it was cold the sun was bright, and the people of the town had bundled up to stroll, or run, or bicycle, or skate by the whipped surface of the water. A mother and father, their boy, who must have been about six, on his bike: the boy's determined face, the helmet perched on his head and strapped under his chin. The mother took the father's hand; the woman said something and the man threw his head back and laughed. The plate glass didn't make for silence, he could hear the sea, and the noise of the people, but nothing was distinct. Once he lifted his hand and felt the cold drift off the glass. Claire's daughter, Stella, was not quite six. Dan had never met Stella and yet, as he sat at the window looking out at the people, the sea, the boy with his parents, it was as if she had run into the room. He had not even seen a photograph of her yet there she was, vivid, long brown hair, pink hairclips, wellington boots and a duffel coat, a grin with one tooth missing, a grin for him. This unknown child, suddenly a bright phantom, running towards him and then vanishing.

No one asked him to move. It was nearly noon when he rose. He might as well go out, he thought. He moved steadily through the hotel, easily. Sometimes it felt to him as if he was gliding, just an inch, or half an inch, above the muted colours of the carpet.

'Dan?'

April. Not much warmer than it had been in March. But not raining. The evenings were lighter; he was walking past the British Museum. He turned.

'Claire.'

'What are you doing here? I thought you lived in Mile End.'

'I do.' They were standing just past the big iron gates, not quite shut, not yet. 'I had to – nothing. You know, get something from one of those shops on Tottenham Court Road. Electronics. A cable.' His heart was beating faster. Did he notice it at the time? She was standing with her feet planted apart; black boots with pointed toes and wedge heels, a neat black macintosh buttoned up to her neck. She was not as tall as he was, but nearly; her eyes were cool and grey, and they looked almost straight into his. They stood for what seemed to him a long time, not speaking. Perhaps it was only a moment, but later, in his memory, he would pull it out, hold it up to the light, the way the threads of grey in her dark hair made him think of feathers, the way she had made up her face, carefully, not as disguise but as – protection, he thought. Tiny diamonds in her ears above the green velvet scarf she wore. 'I liked your paintings,' he said. 'I thought they were the only good things there.'

'That's because they were,' she said, her breath blown out of her flared nostrils, her mouth turned down at its corners. 'It's not saying much.'

'I don't know,' he said. 'What about the tampon thing?' Then she did laugh; they both did. 'Would you like a drink?' he said. 'Or do you have to get home?' Xanthe was at some screening. He did not have to get home.

'No, I don't,' she answered. 'Have to get home. Not yet, anyway.' It was Friday night.

Did it happen then? Did it happen the first time he saw her, standing in front of those deep, obscure oils in the Mayfair gallery? Sometimes he found himself thinking that perhaps it had happened long before that, long before they'd ever met. What idiocy, what lunacy. As if there was destiny, something in the cold stars. There was nothing: only distance, mathematics, a vacuum.

They walked together, in silence, in step. He led her: his

feet took him to a bar he'd been to once, years ago, a place in Soho down a steep flight of stairs. It was dark inside, a low vault with naked brick walls and candles on the table although it was hardly later than afternoon.

'Red or white?' he asked at the bar. The wines were chalked on a board.

'Don't mind. Well, I do really. White,' she said.

He asked for a bottle of Sancerre and pulled out his wallet. The barman, who was very tall with a shaved head and earrings, silently took his £20 note, gave him not much change, the bottle, two glasses, a little bowl of olives; all this they transported to a table.

He didn't know what to say. She was a stranger. Her knee almost touched his. He could have pulled his chair back; so could she. They did not.

'Are you a student?' he said at last. 'An art student?' All the others at the show had been. He knew she wasn't, though; she heard that in his voice. She wasn't like the others, with their spiky hair and rollups – like his students, like Xanthe. At the gallery she'd been quiet. Xanthe had talked about – something. Claire had stood in front of her paintings and watched him, watched them, the room. Shyness, or reserve, he hadn't known.

'No, I'm not,' she said. 'Well, I am, but not full-time, if that's what you mean.' She shook her head. 'This light must be very flattering, if that's what you think.'

He shrugged, embarrassed. It was hard to tell her age. Her face was not beautiful, but neatly made of ordered planes and fine angles. But he looked closely at her now;

again she allowed his gaze, holding his eyes with hers. 'I couldn't stand it, anyway. Being a student. Even when I was one. Well, that was twenty years ago. I've always painted. I thought it would be good to do it in a more structured way; also, I'm making bigger canvases now, and I can keep them at the school.'

'So you . . . ' He didn't know how to frame the question. There was too much he wanted to know.

'I work,' she said. 'I'm a dentist, actually.'

He made a noise. It was a laugh that stopped itself. She looked suddenly solemn.

'What's wrong with that?'

'Nothing, nothing, I . . .'

She had crossed her arms in front of her chest. The nails of her hands were neat, round, unpolished, and she wore no rings.

'Kidding,' she said. 'Don't worry. People seem to be surprised. And they don't know any dentists. But really, I am.' One grey eye closed and opened again.

'And they probably think, oh no, it's been ages since I've been.'

'Generally.'

'Artist–dentist. An unusual combination.'

'Maybe. Or there could be hundreds of us out there. Have you ever asked your dentist what she does in her spare time?'

'His spare time.'

She shrugged.

'I'll have to get home,' she said. 'Not yet, but just to warn you. Nanny's waiting.'

'You have kids?' The feeling of something bursting and deflating. Whatever he had begun to imagine suddenly changed; but she saw, he was sure, what he was thinking. The flame of the candle on their table flinched, jerked a little and guttered, then rose again, straight and clear.

'Stella,' she said. 'My daughter. She's five. It's just the two of us.'

There was no adequate response to this, or not one where the etiquette was available to him. *I'm sorry* was tactless and, in any case, incorrect. In the afternoon, in this dark bar, his wife not many streets away, he was not sorry at all.

He walked out of the hotel and headed not for the promenade but for the main street of the town. This ran parallel to the sea, but back a few blocks: narrow, straight streets where some of the houses were spindly, dark edifices from a story by Edgar Allan Poe, all stained wood and turrets. This place had been popular at the turn of the last century; these faded fantasy mansions were the remnants of that. They were grand no longer. Their paint was bubbling or stripped away by the salt air entirely, clapboards and decorative carving splintered and torn. Some had been pulled down, he guessed, to make way for ugly modern flats with big terraces that looked as if they had been built to overlook the sea, but did not: they faced into the street, only staring at the other ugly modern blocks across from them. Now, in winter, they stared at nothing: steel shutters were rolled down over their faces.

But the main street was pleasant. On a Sunday morning quite a few of the shops were open – the patisserie, the boulangerie, the flower shop, the newsagent's. People carried baskets filled with fruit and vegetables, with bottles, with terrines wrapped in wax paper and tied with string. Everything was pleasingly, but not ostentatiously, displayed behind glass, on tidy shelves; and in front of the flower shop there was a little row of Christmas trees in pots, their branches tied with gingham ribbons. He didn't need to buy anything, of course. He would eat at the hotel – or somewhere else – or not eat at all. When he was on his own, lately, he often didn't bother until he discovered he was so hungry he had a headache, or felt ill. The rhythms of his life had gone and he did not feel moved to replace them; he couldn't see what there was to replace them with. Sometimes, for an instant, he could imagine a possibility of something; it could be as simple as a scent. Just now, as he walked, it happened: a quick whiff of frying, of *frites*, and the drift of hot oil brought saliva to his mouth and made him feel as if this could be what he wanted, that it might be this easy. And then the odour vanished, and so did the desire.

At the newsagent's he stopped to buy cigarettes. It had been a long time since he smoked. He stood behind the counter for a while, staring up at what seemed, for a small shop in a small town, a vast selection of tobacco of every variety. '*M'sieur?*' the woman behind the counter asked him. She was tall and pale, thick red hair pulled back in a plait.

'Ah – *un moment*,' he said. His French was not very good at all. She nodded, and went back to leafing through a magazine. A man moved past him, and the woman looked up to sell him three postcards and a pack of gum; someone else came in and bought a newspaper, a woman with a little boy in tow. The boy was about four, he guessed; wore a coat with a velvet collar. *Stella.*

The woman with the boy left. The door banged; a draught of freezing air blew by. It took a minute for him to be able to speak, and then he said, '*Mademoiselle . . .*' and the woman looked up from her magazine. '*Un paquet – les cigares . . .*' He pointed. More interesting than cigarettes. He saw a little wooden box shut with a brass clasp, a pattern of stars scattered on the label: *Les Pléiades.*

She stood on tiptoes to reach the box, took it down, set the cigars down on the counter. 'Eight euros,' she said, in English.

'Thank you,' he said, feeling absurdly grateful, not for the cigars, but for her two English words.

She shrugged, smiled a little also, and put two single euros in his palm. She did not touch him: her fingers touched the metal, the metal touched his hand. 'You are from England?' she said, and he nodded. 'They all go home by now, I thought,' she said. 'After *le weekend.*'

'I'm staying,' he said. 'Just for a day or so.'

'I don't know why,' she said bluntly. 'There is nothing to do around here.'

'Oh, I don't know,' he said. 'I like to walk by the sea. It's good to be away.' To tell the truth to strangers.

'Even stupid things are interesting when they are not yours,' the woman said. 'I guess that's how it is. You probably think England is not so good. I would like to go.'

The door banged. A teenage girl, dyed black hair, orange lipstick. She tried to buy some cigarettes. The woman behind the counter said something that sounded like *chut*, tossed her head so her thick plait flipped over her shoulder, and the girl scuttled off. 'You've never been?' Dan asked.

'No,' the woman said. Her eyes were dark brown and there was a fan of lines at their corners where the skin was a little paler, just inside the thin creases. She had a smattering of freckles across the broad bridge of her nose. 'Only over there,' she gestured towards where the sea would be, through the back of the shop. 'Ridiculous.'

Then there was nothing more to say. He could have said something, of course. Anything. Now the possibility of *anything* was no longer what it had been to him. 'I need – a lighter,' he said.

The woman took one from a thicket of them that stood beside the till. She held it up. '*Le briquet*,' she said. She did not hand it over. He realised he was expected to repeat what she'd said.

'*Le briquet*,' he gave her. '*Merci*.'

She handed it over and he reached in his pocket for some change, but she shook her head. '*De rien*,' she said. 'You don't smoke, do you?'

'Not for a while.'

She nodded. He wished he had a hat; he would have liked to tip it to her, at least. He put his hand on the smooth brass knob of the door. '*Attention*,' she said at his back, 'if you walk at the sea. The tide comes in fast.'

He told Xanthe because Claire had gone. It was, he knew now, he knew at the time, he knew for all eternity, a very foolish thing to have done. Xanthe had trusted him; had suspected nothing, discovered nothing; and now that Claire had left she never would. But the secret – no, worse than the secret, the loss – sat in his heart like some horned beast that had climbed inside him, tearing at him from within, desperate to get out. What he'd swallowed when they'd first kissed, hidden beneath her tongue, an incubus. They'd met for lunch one afternoon in a cheap Indian restaurant near her office, by the Euston Road. She was quiet and reserved. She said it quickly, first thing, something to get over with. *I've met someone else.*

He just stopped himself from saying So? Or: But I *live* with someone else. He said nothing. He listened, though he did not hear, not really, only the noise his blood seemed to be making, sloshing around pointlessly in his head.

'I like you,' she'd said. 'I like you a lot. But you . . . '

'Yes.' There was no case to make. Yet he had begun to feel: what? Entitled. It had nothing to do with Claire, nothing to do with Xanthe. It was his own life, and now it was being spoiled. Some opportunity had passed him by. He was angry. He had not been given a chance. He could have been asked to choose. In that instant, he imagined clearly the life he had never been offered: Stella's warm little hand in his own, the idea so bright that Claire herself nearly vanished. Yet that had never been part of it. What had happened between them had been meant to be plain. Simple. And then she'd said: 'It's just . . . '

He didn't speak into her pause. He waited.

'You can't do that – and not feel something.' She wasn't looking at him, she was looking at the table, dragging her finger through a drop of spilt water. It was only later he'd thought to wonder (over and over) of whom she spoke. Of him? Or perhaps she meant this other, that she felt for him now and could not betray him. It galled him, this latter thought, almost beyond repair. She'd kissed him when they'd parted; squeezed his fingers with her own. Keep in touch, she'd said. Yes, he'd said again, wondering if this was only the next lie.

So he went home. He continued. He cooked the dinner and kept himself a smooth surface, as if Xanthe could skate over him, happily. And she had not asked. She had not guessed. But one night she put her hand on the back of his neck, just for an instant, her palm just above the collar of his shirt, and he had said: 'I'm sorry.'

She laughed. 'Sorry for what?'

He had told her.

Did he think this would make it go away, kill it, the thing inside him, the beast? He must have. There were, he recalled, at least several seconds at the beginning of his narration when he felt a certain relief. It did not last.

Xanthe did not shout or weep. 'You know,' she said a few nights later, sitting again in the kitchen, each of them in front of a plate of untouched risotto which he had cooked like a machine, stirring and stirring as if some solution were hidden at the bottom of a cast-iron pan, 'I don't mind that you fucked her. I mind that you love her. And you know why I mind that?' She looked straight at him. Her eyes were green with flecks of amber at the edges of the pupils; her brows were straight and thick. All of her was in there, he'd always thought, in the emphatic strokes of her eyebrows, clean as water in their darkness, certain and true. She had been twenty-four when they met, full of the fugitive swiftness of youth, like quicksilver; but there was more than that, there was the elemental solidity of her too, a mercurial density and strength. Eight years, they had been together; six years married. He wouldn't have thought it was so long. Time had gone quickly. Time flies when you're having fun. 'I mind because you don't *know* her. How could you love someone you don't know? You have a crush on her, you fancy her, you want to—' She stopped. 'But love? And so I think, what does that say about you? Who are you, who can love what he doesn't even know? Not anyone I want. Maybe no one I ever knew.'

He hadn't thought that she wouldn't care, or, indeed, that she might offer to heal him. But he could not forgive her (because he knew he could not forgive himself) the weight of her old-fashioned scorn. He had not told her about Stella. He was afraid to. After her rage, he knew what she might say: I could have a baby. We could have a baby now. But he did not want that baby. Some baby as yet unmade, previously unconsidered (they had their lives, their work, they were still young, or at least, Xanthe was), only now made present in the world to which he no longer belonged. Claire was not his secret now. Stella, the unknown Stella, he would keep.

After that first, great alteration of the pressure between them there was no dramatic split or fracture. His treasure dropped out of his grasp and he did not bend to catch it, perceiving it to be tarnished and changed. Even when Xanthe talked about moving out – she could go to her sister's, to her big house in Clapham with its tenantless attic flat – the image of Claire, liquid, translucent, would float in front of his eyes. The dip at her collarbone, a mauve shadow, her head turned to the side on a cheap foam pillow, her eyes closed. The sole of her foot against the palm of his hand. The small of her back raised in yellow light from the street outside, her shoulders thrown forward, dark threads of hair at the nape of her neck, her soft belly with its faint dark line, Stella's mark, and the silver streaks at her hips that made him think of a mermaid. He thought he tried to push these pictures away, but when they began to fade he realised he would rehearse them, over and over, trying to make them sharp again, trying to make them clear. But they dropped away, drowned in the water of time, blurring; and then Xanthe began to drop away too. And so, he was alone.

*

When he awoke, it was dark. Was it the middle of the night? He must have fallen asleep in his clothes, then. The clock on the mirror-topped vanity across from him flashed its red eye: 5:30. In the morning? It couldn't be. He had not slept for fifteen hours. No: he had slept for three hours, and it was 5:30 in the afternoon, pitch black because it was the middle of winter.

His back hurt, his legs hurt when he got out of the bed. He took his bones to the bathroom and leaned his head on the cool tiles while he pissed, the waterfall noise echoing in the tiny box of the room. Washed his hands, brushed his teeth again. Coat on again. Dinner: he should eat, he should eat something. Out the door again. It was amazing how life was like that, this series of repetitions, like it was all practice for something.

He turned left out of the hotel – the clerk now back at his place before the glowing rows of bottles – and down towards the sea. He would eat at the hotel, yes, but it was too early to eat. He could see the promenade at the end of the straight street: just a slice of it, but he could tell it was empty now, early on a Sunday evening; between the façades of two tall houses no one passed, no cyclists or rollerskaters. Even the sea was quieter: the tide must be out. He remembered the cigars in his pocket. He hadn't smoked one yet. He pulled out the wooden box, flicked open the catch, pulled out the narrow brown cylinder and set it between his lips. *Le briquet.* Cupping his hands around the flame, his back curved, the bitter smoke dark in his mouth. He blew it out into the wind, and on the wind that blew back at him was the music of an organ.

He walked slowly, listening. It was easy to follow, the sound: just down the block, halfway between the hotel and the sea. One house with lit windows, and as he approached he slowed and then stood still, not in front, not directly, but just to the side of the big sash window, wide plates of glass with watery edges.

Panels of dark wood. A wooden table, also dark, and set, he saw, if he stood just on his toes, for two, with silver and pale linen mats. An arrangement of flowers on the table in a plain glass vase shaped like a pear. On one wall, a dark portrait, of a woman in black with a white kerchief or head-dress on her head, her small stiff hands folded in her lap, her mouth a straight line. The frame gilt against the dark wood. And, against the far wall, the organ and a man with a straight back and silver hair before it, his body moving slightly as his hands, which Dan couldn't see, passed over the keyboard. The little organ played lightly, sweetly, almost as if it were singing: it was not like a church organ. The notes passed through the glass and out to the street, out to Dan, who stood, not minding the cold, listening.

Then the man playing the organ stopped, turned his head: he had heard something, perhaps, that Dan had not. And then – Dan almost laughed – there was the woman, the woman from the newsagent's, with her straightforward face and long red hair, carrying a tray into the panelled room. He could see a bottle of wine, two covered china dishes; she set them down on the table and the man at the organ looked at her. Dan could see his face now. He was older than the woman: old enough to be her father, and he might have been, or he might not. She had put the tray down now, both of them in profile to him, and he could see those little fans at the corners of her eyes, the web of lines spreading as she looked at the man, as they looked at each other. What passed between them made him take a step forward, as if it could be his too, as if there were no glass between this warm room and where he stood.

For a moment he wondered if he might have knocked. There was the door, painted black, a fat brass ring. What would the expression on her face have been? He stood in front of it and thought of it opened, his foot over the threshold, a quick embrace, as if he were visiting old friends, an entire life he did not know he had until he'd stood in this night, in this street, the wind from the sea down his collar, his feet at the edge of the thrown glow of sodium light.

Dan stepped away from the window and down towards the water. The little cigar was dead in his stiff hand; he threw it down into the gutter. At the promenade he did not turn, did not walk along it, but went down the steps that led to the beach because he could see that the tide was indeed out, the sea so far away he could have believed it had receded entirely, off the edge of the world. The sand was hard under the soles of his shoes, with hardly any give at all, though occasionally his step would splash in an eddy of water than had carved a hard-edged canyon through it.

It was then that he saw it again, or felt it. The same thing he'd felt this morning, sitting at the breakfast table in the hotel with croissant crumbs in his lap and cold coffee in front of him. The same sink in his belly, the drop, when he'd caught sight of – he stopped dead. He looked out. The moon was a sliver, a blink of light, giving nothing away. But out there, where there was water, shallow water, lapping against rock or wood or a wreck, some change in its shape and then this gaze that reached him. He would have to call it that. No eyes, but the sense of eyes. A dark shape, a head, not a shadow on the water, but something he could see and touch if he could reach it, if he could walk in the dark and leave behind what had gone before. This was the threshold, the door. He heard music again: the organ, of course, the faint thread of it reaching him. He put one foot in front of the other and kept walking on the hard sand, through the salt pools, out towards the rocks and the distant sea.

THE CALLING

ALLAN WEISBECKER

The Springs, Long Island, New York, 1922

MALCOLM STEWART HAD LOST account of how long he'd been curled up under the seine net but it sure seemed like forever. His legs'd cramped up on him and no matter which way he adjusted himself, something – a cork float or a lead or a knot or *something* – would poke him in a way that hurt, especially when the wagon hit a rut in the road and the dory shifted in about five directions at once.

The twine was damp and frosty from overnight dew and its cold weight made Malcolm shiver. He wished he'd thought to wear his heavier sweater, but when you're all warm in bed you tend to forget what it's like outside before dawn in late October. He'd other things to think about, too, like the beating he was going to get when Papa found him. Malcolm hoped that'd be after they'd gone off and were outside the sand bar and Papa wouldn't go back to the beach just to put him ashore.

Malcolm wanted to stretch his legs, maybe work the cramps loose, but Scun Bennett was sitting up in the bow chewing tobacco and Malcolm didn't want to take the chance at being found, especially by Scun. Malcolm'd had a fight with Danny Boy Bennett, Scun's nephew, the week before and'd kicked Danny Boy all over the schoolyard, making him cry in front of everybody, so Malcolm'd taken to avoiding the Bennett men, which wasn't easy since there was about a million of them between Southampton and Montauk.

The Stewarts and Bennetts had never gotten along, never even married one another, not in over two hundred years, going on three hundred, of being neighbours, and Malcolm figured if Scun happened to find him he'd probably give Malcolm a kick in the head and claim it was an accident. (Malcolm also figured Scun was feeling the gaff about having to ride in the dory instead of up in the wagon, but it was Papa's rig and Scun didn't have a choice in the matter.) But Malcolm wished Scun'd quit farting every time they bounced, making Malcolm clinch his teeth so he wouldn't laugh.

Malcolm heard Papa say Hoooo! and old Left Eye whinnied and pulled up; they must be at the Lester place. Through a fold in the seine Malcolm could see Scun sitting up on the bow thwart and even in the dim starlight made out the knot of chew in his cheek as he looked for the Lester brothers to come out of the house.

Malcolm heard hinges creak and a door slam, then the crunch of boots on the sand and broken clam and scallop shells on the Lesters' front lawn. Old Left Eye snorted and Papa called out, 'If you boys don't pick 'em up and lay 'em down a little faster, the Edwards boys'll catch all the fish in the damn ocean and then where will we be?'

Malcolm felt the dory shift and groan on the trailer as

one of the brothers, probably Ted – he was younger than Bill by a good bit and'd have to ride in the back with Scun – climbed on up and when he threw his legs over the gunwale and down into the dory his left boot came down no more'n a foot from Malcolm's face.

'Mornin', Scun.' It was Ted all right.

Please don't sit on the net, sit on the thwart, Malcolm thought, but it didn't work. Ted sat right down on the seine and Malcolm thought he'd cry out from Ted's weight. Ted shifted around and tried to make himself comfortable, and Malcolm's breath slowly leaked out of him. Then Ted commenced bouncing up and down with his rear end, trying to make an indentation that would fit it. Each time Ted bounced Malcolm felt more air going out and a little moan along with it, which he couldn't help, but neither Ted nor Scun heard him.

Finally Ted got up and sat back down on the midships thwart where he should have sat to start with. He said something about the twine being too damp and lumpy to sit on while Malcolm breathed in shallow gasps; he wondered if this was the way a striped bass felt, lying in the bottom of the dory with his mouth and gills moving as he drowned in the air.

Meanwhile, Papa'd said Yooo! and the wagon was moving again. It'd soon turn onto the highway, which was a lot smoother and'd someday be paved like it was up in Southampton, or at least that's what everyone said, though Papa doubted it and so did Malcolm.

Malcolm's breath was coming easier now but the

cramps in his legs were even worse and the cold felt deeper, down in his bones. Then, suddenly, his teeth started chattering.

'What in 'ell is that?' It was Ted, who was only maybe four feet away, and his voice sounded like it was coming from inside Malcolm's head, it was that loud and clear in the cool, windless morning.

'What was what?' Scun was further away, working his chew and spitting about every two seconds. He was a noisy fella in general and didn't tend to pick up on things. But Ted, Ted paid attention to the goings-on around him.

'That clickin' sound.' Malcolm felt the seine stir; Ted was poking around. 'Sounds like something in the twine.'

Malcolm gritted his teeth to stop the chattering. Scun spat and said, 'Prob'ly a crab clickin' his claws,' then they hit a deep rut and Scun farted something spectacular. Malcolm almost laughed and thought maybe he'd made a noise trying to hold it in. He found it hilarious when grown-ups farted.

Then suddenly there was Ted's face, sideways, and he was looking into Malcolm's eyes. Even in the near darkness Malcolm could see Ted was surprised to find Tom Stewart's kid hiding under the seine.

Now Malcolm figured he wouldn't get to go fishing this morning and'd have to put up with the beating too. But Ted didn't say anything. He just stared at Malcolm and now instead of looking surprised he was looking curious, his brow all furrowed and lower lip sticking out in a comical way. 'Yep, you're right, Scun,' Ted called out. 'It's a crab clickin' his claws in 'ere!'

Malcolm was so surprised he let fly a bout of teeth chattering right into Ted's face. It was so loud Ted laughed, and it went on and on and got louder and louder until Scun told Ted to kill the goddamn thing; he'd finally heard the racket over his chewing and farting. Ted said Okay then reached into the seine and covered Malcolm's mouth until the chattering passed. He called out to Scun that he'd killed the damn crab, ripped his claw off good, then his face disappeared but he put his boot, the right one this time, down in the bottom of the dory where Malcolm could see it. Then Ted started up a conversation with Scun and Malcolm listened. 'Amazing that crab survived in the twine since yesterday,' he said.

'Tom Stewart don't take care to clean his 'quipment,' Scun said, but he kept his voice down, no doubt so Papa, driving the rig, wouldn't hear. 'Otherwise 'ere wouldn't be no crab in 'ere.'

Ted said, 'The Stewarts is overrated as fishermen, if you was to ask me,' and he tapped his boot on the dory's planking to let Malcolm know he was trying to stir Scun up so Malcolm'd be in on it. Malcolm knew that Ted, all the Lesters in fact, had nothing but respect for Papa, as a fisherman and neighbour both.

Scun said, 'Goddamn right they's overrated,' but he sure was keeping his voice low.

Malcolm was pleased as could be about what was going on. Ted was almost a grown-up – he was fifteen and had been on Papa's haul seine crew since the spring – and here he was sharing a rib with Malcolm, who wasn't even close to being a grown-up, and hadn't been fishing, at least not real fishing, ever.

Malcolm didn't figure he had any close friends, aside from Willie Long and maybe that girl Rosie, but Malcolm *hated* her, and he pictured for a moment how great it'd be if Ted became his friend and ally.

Ted tapped his boot again to let Malcolm know the conversation would soon get hilarious. Ted said, 'I heard Malcolm Stewart and your nephew went at it the other day at school over whether the Bennetts or the Stewarts is better fishermen.'

Scun said, 'Yup, and Danny Boy beat hell out of the little sonofabitch.'

Malcolm came so close to saying something that a squeak leaked out but Ted coughed real loud to drown it and tapped his boot like mad, so Malcolm held his tongue.

Then Ted said, 'Why don't you and your brothers start up your own crew, Scun? Show them Stewarts how to set an ocean seine for striped bass?'

Scun said, 'Been thinkin' 'bout it,' but Malcolm could tell Scun'd never thought about it, never in his life.

Ted said, 'Me an' Bill, we was talkin' jus' the other night 'bout how we'd rather fish with you than Tom Stewart any time.' Ted didn't tap his boot on *that* comment; he was probably too busy trying to keep himself from laughing at the ridiculousness of it.

Malcolm could hear Scun working his chew like crazy

and spitting and no doubt thinking about what it'd be like to have his own rig and crew. Then he said, real huffy, 'Maybe I will do just that.'

Malcolm heard the squeak of the trailer hitch and old Left Eye snorted again and the clop-clop of his hooves changed their rhythm. He felt the dory shift and lean a little and knew they'd turned onto the highway. Ted called up to Papa, 'Where do you figger we'll make the daybreak set, Tom?'

Papa called back, 'Down in front of the Napeague shanty, 'less someone got a theory what makes more sense.'

Ted said, 'Sounds 'bout right to me,' then he lowered his voice and said, 'What do *you* think, Scun?' He tapped his boot.

Malcolm grinned. Scun didn't know one piece of ocean from the other, but Ted had gotten him all worked up with the thought of having his own crew and Malcolm wondered if Scun'd come up with something stupid.

He did. He said, 'Maybe a little further east, Tom.'

Well, Papa said Hooo! and actually pulled up, he was so surprised Scun'd said that. It got real quiet and Scun stopped working his chew and spitting and Malcolm knew Papa was squinting at Scun, waiting for him to explain his theory of going further east to make the daybreak set.

Malcolm knew Scun had absolutely no theory about anything and it took all his will power to keep from busting a gut. Ted was tapping his boot to let Malcolm know the situation was even funnier from where he was sitting.

It was Malcolm who let Scun off the hook but Malcolm couldn't help it. His teeth erupted in a chattering fit, so loud this time that even Papa heard it, up in the wagon. Papa said, 'What's that noise?'

Scun's voice went deep, like he was in charge of the goings-on back in the dory. 'It's a goddamn crab in the twine, Tom.' Then he got even more serious, like it was *dangerous* or something to have a crab running loose in the seine, and he said, 'I *told* Ted here to kill damn thing.' You could tell Scun was mainly relieved that the subject of going further east to make the daybreak set had gotten changed.

Ted mumbled he was sorry for not obeying Scun, then there he was again, squinting at Malcolm through a fold in the twine. It was closer to morning now and Malcolm could see Ted was all wound up tight from trying not to laugh.

Ted yelled out, 'It's another crab, Scun, a big 'un!' and he stuck his hand in the seine and grabbed Malcolm's coat, flopping around like he was in a battle to the death with a monster crab from prehistoric times.

Malcolm's teeth wouldn't stop chattering so Ted stuffed a piece of the cork line into Malcolm's mouth to deaden the sound. Ted yelled, 'I kilt 'im, Scun!' then backed himself out of the seine.

Malcolm bit down hard on the cork line and silent laughter came in waves that shook his body. Malcolm was cold and his legs hurt and he expected a beating, but he didn't think he'd ever felt as good as he did at that moment, sharing a rib with Ted Lester at the expense of Scun Bennett.

Malcolm felt old Left Eye straining and his snorting and louder breathing and the heavier feel of the trailer meant they'd reached the soft sand of Napeague Beach.

The air was different, too. It wasn't any colder than it'd been on the road but it breathed in crisper and made your thoughts clearer and more hopeful. The beach and the ocean did that to the air.

Malcolm tried to picture where they might be. He saw in his mind the Stewarts' fish shanty – first built by Great-great-grandpa Joshua and rebuilt after storm surges by subsequent generations – in its dune nook, driftwood fashioned, battered and blasted and scoured and bleached by the sun, sea and wind-whipped sand. He saw the rig toiling on by the shanty to the spot where Papa, by habit, liked to stop for a look-see at what the ocean was up to in the mornings.

Malcolm thought about Napeague Beach, how the Stewarts past and present felt a kinship for the wild fragility of its windswept dune hills and the delicate life that somehow flourished on those arid, salty slopes. He thought of Grandpa Eli, gone now, or as the old man'd say, Shifted Yonder; how he'd explained that nothing more permanent or disturbing than a shanty should be struck upon dunes, not ever. It was hurtful, the harassment of dunes, and Grandpa Eli saw them, as with the Indians he'd shore-whaled with, as magical things to be touched only lightly and with respect.

Malcolm heard old Left Eye whinny, and finding he'd closed his eyes to better see times and people not of the present, opened them and squinted through the web of the seine. He could see Ted and Scun pretty clearly now, daybreak wasn't far off, and they were both looking up ahead and not saying anything.

A seagull flew over and Malcolm heard him cry out, likely ruffled at the intrusion of men into his fine domain. Papa said Hooo! and pulled up. Old Left Eye whinnied again and Malcolm felt him shifting around nervously, which was unusual. He was an old horse and a calm one.

Then Malcolm too got a nervous feeling, a deeper sensation than the cold or even the fear of Papa's anger, and suddenly Malcolm knew what it was, and why the men were so quiet.

The waves'd come up big during the night and the men were watching them roll in.

Malcolm focused on the sound of the ocean. At first it was like a fire burning too hot in the belly of the kitchen stove after you'd put in too much green wood. It was a roaring and a hissing like that. Then there'd be a crack, like a log splitting open, and the hissing would get louder as the insides of the wood caught. Malcolm figured that was the sound of a wave breaking on the outside bar and charging in towards the beach. The hissing would fade as the white water died in the depths between the bar and the beach. Then another outside wave would break and the rhythm would repeat itself.

Then there was a heavy sound, like the thud of someone

far off blowing a stump, and it made Malcolm's heart pound. It'd seemed to rise up from below, up from the beach, up through the wagon and the dory, and it was the earth itself shaking from the power of a wave when there was no more water to carry it and it fell onto the sand. Malcolm put his hand on the dory's cedar planking and felt the ocean stirring and angry there in the wood.

Then Scun Bennett spoke and his words seemed directed at Malcolm. Scun said, 'We shoulda stayed in bed.' The tremor in Scun's voice made Malcolm shiver and he felt Scun's fear.

Ted didn't say anything and neither did Papa nor Bill.

Again the thud, louder and harder and deeper, and the oar on the portside vibrated and the blade slipped off the thwart and fell into the bottom of the dory. Old Left Eye snorted and shifted around and Papa said Easy boy to settle him.

Scun said, 'It's too big to go out, Tom,' and Malcolm was hoping Papa'd say, You're right, Scun. But Malcolm'd never seen Papa afraid and he couldn't imagine it, not now, not ever, no matter how big the waves got.

Papa said, 'Seems fishy out there.' Some said Papa had a way with the striped bass, a way of knowing when they were nearby, like Grandpa Eli'd had with cod, even though he'd claimed the right whale as *his fish*. (Malcolm believed the schoolbooks were right about the whale not being a fish, but he kept it to himself, out of respect for his ancestor, who was no longer around to argue the point.)

Malcolm remembered Grandpa Eli's thoughts on the

matter of certain Stewart men knowing when fish were about when there were no outward signs of their presence, a subject of much debate amongst the clan. It was a gift, the old man'd said, like being able to navigate the dream world rather than just being tossed around in it, which he claimed the Indians could do. Papa'd argued that that notion was a doryful of nonsense and maybe even blasphemous, and pointed out that if a man knew there were fish out there, it was because there were outward signs, even if the fellow was only half aware of them. Papa'd gotten riled in his opinion on this but Grandpa Eli hadn't said anything back. He'd just looked at Malcolm and winked in a strange way, like he and Malcolm shared something apart from Papa.

Hiding there under the seine, Malcolm felt himself shiver, and it was not from the cold. It was from the recollection of Grandpa Eli's wink.

Ted bent over and fiddled with his boot. He looked at Malcolm and whispered, 'Your dad's thinkin' 'bout goin' off. If I was you I'd sneak myself outta there and run myself home while ever'body's lookin' sea'ard. Thim waves's big.'

Malcolm didn't want Ted to know he was afraid so he shook his head, but in his mind he saw himself running for the dunes. He shook his head harder to rid himself of that picture and kept right on shaking it as Ted frowned, but Ted's eyes were bright, like he was excited about what Malcolm was doing.

As Ted straightened up and looked seaward again, at the

waves Malcolm felt but couldn't see, Papa said, 'Come on, boys, let's give it a try.'

Bill said, 'All right, Tom,' but he didn't sound real eager about the prospect.

Malcolm looked at Scun. It was light enough now to see his face clearly as he turned from the ocean and looked back towards the dunes. He said, 'I don't know, Tom.' Scun spat but hardly anything came out.

Ted said, 'I'll go. You tend to shore this time, Scun,' and Ted *did* sound eager. He was the youngest of any of the haul seine crews and Malcolm figured he was hot to prove himself.

Papa said, 'Okay then. Let's go.'

Ted sprang over the gunwale and Malcolm heard him land on the sand. Scun got out much slower and said, 'I don't know,' as he lowered himself onto the beach.

Malcolm felt the wagon lurch and groan as Papa turned the rig towards the water. Old Left Eye whinnied real loud and Papa said Easy to get him to back down but old Left Eye didn't want to go closer to the waves shaking the earth under his hooves.

Papa said Okay boy then Malcolm felt the stern lift under him and the men were grunting and the dory was moving, sliding off the trailer with a terrible scraping and Malcolm's heart pounded at the sound of it. He felt her ease down then fall hard onto the rollers and the side of his face hurt from smacking the planks as it landed.

Papa said, 'Those waves's comin' in threes, boys,' and the rumble of the ocean deepened and echoed in the bottom of the dory. There was a gurgling and Malcolm felt the wash rush up and the dory moved a little on the rollers. Scun Bennett tried to spit, it sounded dry, and said, 'I don't know, Tom. This don't seem worth it to me.'

Papa dealt with Scun's opinion by saying, 'Let's wet her, boys,' and Malcolm felt the dory sliding over the rollers then onto the sand. The bow dropped and she was sliding easier, down the steep slope and into the shallows where suddenly she was free of the beach and Malcolm was aware of the hands all around on the gunwales, steadying her movements in the spent white water.

Ted climbed back in, joined now by Bill, and Malcolm saw their boots through the seine as they unshipped oars up forward and the locks creaked as the brothers set up their rhythm.

No one spoke as Papa and Bill and Ted and Scun – Malcolm could hear their hard breathing all around – waited for a slatch, a lull in the cycle of the waves.

Then Papa yelled, 'Go, boys!' and Malcolm felt the dory moving seaward and Papa and Scun were pushing her and the Lesters were pulling hard for the outside and with each oar stroke Malcolm's fear rose and tightened.

'Pull, boys! Pull!' Papa was in the dory now, standing aft by the net and the oars banged in the locks as Ted and Bill pulled. Malcolm could see Ted's face through the twine, against the reddening morning sky, and Ted was straining as Papa called out, 'Pull, boys!'

'Put your backs into it, boys!' and Ted somehow pulled even harder, his lean body rising off the thwart, back angling towards the bow with each stroke, eyes intent on Papa, as spray from the bow and splash from the oar blades rained down. Then the dory struck a wall of white water and she shuddered, every plank and rib of her, and Malcolm shuddered too, at the might of the sea.

Above the pounding and the roaring Papa's cry rose again, 'Please pull for me, boys!' and Malcolm knew that danger lay ahead on the shoal of the bar.

'Pull, boys! Pull *harder*!' and water was rising in the bottom of the dory and Malcolm felt a warmth spreading down there and he knew he'd wet his pants from the chill and the fear.

'Pull, pull for your lives, boys!' and the rush of the water and the banging of the oars and the Lesters' fierce breathing and Papa's hollering were so loud Malcolm thought his ears would burst.

The bow was rising now and there was a slowness to it, as if the dory were climbing a mountain of such towering loft that there was no hurry, and the water up forward flowed aft and sloshed into Malcolm's mouth as he tried to cry out for help. Malcolm's eyes roamed wild and fretful and they found Ted through the tangle of the twine but even in his panic Malcolm knew that Ted could not help him, not now, for their only hope lay in Ted and Bill's muscles, in their will to Pull!, to Pull *hard* and take them beyond the wave to the safety of the deep outside the bar.

Up further the dory rose, up that mountain wave, she was nearly vertical now and Malcolm could feel her, with each pull from the Lesters, trying to burst over the steepening mass of moving ocean, but she had so far to go to reach the top.

Malcolm felt himself sliding aft and with a great clamouring and banging and yelling, men and gear, a boot, an oar, a bucket were all mixed together in the seine and Malcolm tried to cry out he was sorry for the bad things he'd done in his life but no words would come. Malcolm heard Papa over the outcry and tumult and Papa was saying, 'By God, boys,' his voice dispirited now, and somewhere Mama was crying for her young son, gone now, lost at sea.

Malcolm opened his eyes. He was gripping the left gunwale and he was free from the seine. Over the easterly horizon, the freshly risen sun shined ever so bright and Ted and Bill were stroking the dory through its golden wake.

The dazzling light and sudden expanse of unbroken sea made Malcolm blink. As the fog in his mind lifted, he realised that the Lesters' last desperate oar stroke had propelled the dory over the back of that rogue wave and the impact on the calm water behind it had flipped the seine, freeing him from its snarly grasp.

Then Malcolm felt Papa's arms around him and he wondered why Papa was hugging him so hard and why Papa was saying Sorry, son, when Papa should have been beating him for what he'd done, for hiding under the seine. Papa shook his head. 'Scun was right, boys,' he said, and his eyes were sorrowful. 'It weren't a day to go off.'

A silence fell over them and as it grew so grew a

sensation in Malcolm, unlike any he'd ever felt or imagined. It started as a tingling in his scalp, which spread downward until his body seemed all awash in a faint electric charge. This faded, dissolving into a general sense of well-being and optimism, which itself grew, and it was stronger than his thankfulness at being delivered from the sea's cold clutch with his bones unbroken; stronger even than his love for Papa and Mama and Grandpa Eli, Shifted Yonder now. The feeling surged and swelled and as Malcolm stared down at the gently rolling blue, his mind was transfixed but clear in its purpose, in *his* purpose.

He had to see to the setting of the seine, for striped bass were stirring the depths, unseen, all around him, moving as one and whispering a hushed shimmering sweetness Malcolm heard and understood.

READING CONNEMARA'S COASTLINE

JOSEPH O'CONNOR

WHEN I WAS A BOY in the suburban Dublin of the 1970s, my father used to take us on holiday to Connemara. It was a region of western Ireland we loved, a wonderland of delights. Summer would arrive and the talk would turn quickly to the matter of when we would make for the west. The preparations, the small rituals of the annual pilgrimage, simply became part of our lives.

The Atlantic was the essence of Connemara's allure. At home in Dun Laoghaire we lived near the coast, but our local version, for all its charms, seemed tame. We had ice-cream vans, a public baths, a forlorn chipper – Gene Vincent on the jukebox, the Virgin Mary on the wall. Old ladies shuffled along the pier, arm in arm, tutting at the greasers and their bell-bottomed babes. But it wasn't the real thing. It was Brighton with nuns. You could walk from Glasthule all the way to Booterstown and scarcely set eyes on a grain of sand.

You didn't see the waves roar in from the horizon, those thunderous breakers born off Newfoundland, or feel the shocking tang of spray in your mouth. In Dublin we had the sea. In Connemara they had the ocean. We were the Wombles. They were the Stones.

If Connemara's history is a ghost story, its phantoms are sea-ghosts. Grace O'Malley of Inishbofin, the pirate queen, who forced the mighty Elizabeth I to learn Gaelic so as to be able to address her. The smugglers who took refuge in the coves of Ballynahinch, safe from the muskets of prowling revenue agents. The Princess of Connemara, Mary Martin, her fame sung in novels, the beauty of her age, who voyaged to New York only to die in a cheap hotel. Cartography includes such phantoms, and many more. The gazetteer accompanying Tim Robinson's magnificent map of Connemara is both masterpiece of linguistic archaeology and roll-call of the departed. Scailp Johnny: the grotto that hid an outlaw from the yeomanry in 1798. Lochán na hOinsí: the foolish woman's lake. Meall an tSaighdiúra: the hummock of the soldier; landscape's commemoration of an unnamed English trooper who died after profaning a holy well. This coastline seemed to me then, as it seems to me still, a storybook of spectres waiting to be opened.

Yet for all its familiarity, Connemara felt exotic. I remember sitting in the back of my father's Hillman Hunter on those wearisome, annual westward drives, reading the place-names of coastal Connemara from his fraying AA roadmap. Bunnahown, Rosroe, Kilkerrin, Tawnaghbaun, Aillenacally, Aillebrack, Curhownagh, Ardnagreevagh. If you said them aloud the result was poetry. What would these havens be like when we saw them again? Could they possibly be as beautiful as their mellifluous names? For how ethereal that vowelly geography sounded, how thrilling its music on a Dublin tongue. To speak it you had to use every muscle in your mouth. It gave you the feeling that language was love.

It was on one of those blissful childhood jaunts into Connemara that we stopped at the village of Letterfrack. I can remember the moment I first set foot in the place, with my father, Seán, in about 1972. Three decades have passed, but whenever I drive through Letterfrack now, I am struck once again by its strange appeal. It's a neat little hamlet, not far from the coast, with thatched cottages, cosy pubs; chocolate-box pretty. An aroma of the sea drifts in on the air, commingling with that Connemara redolence of peat-smoke and rain. Turf stacks are silhouetted on the stony hillsides. Trawlers churn the whitecaps off nearby White Strand.

Not far from the town is the manor where Yeats honeymooned. Close by is the ruined grave of one Commander Blake, a nineteenth-century landlord despised by his tenants. (He appears in my novel, *Star of the Sea*.) His tomb, in the weedy rubble of a long-deserted Protestant chapel, overlooks a seaside campsite on the outskirts of Renvyle. Near by you can stroll on a shingled beach. Sea-wrack, gull-call, Atlantic breezes – the eerie loveliness of certain Irish coastal places. There is a sense of continuities, of things unchanged for generations. But all this is illusory, the wishful thinking of the interloper. Modernity has indeed touched Letterfrack. *Father Ted* might be playing on the TV in the bar. The guesthouses offer en suite bathrooms, as well as turf fires.

We tourists take pleasure in the emptiness of Connemara, its remorselessly jagged coastland, its broken-down piers. We don't think of unemployment, emigration, rural poverty. For centuries the fantasies of outsiders have been projected onto this place. It has been Connemara's lot to be regarded as a repository of authenticity, and it struggles, still, to be what we want. Our feet crunch its beaches; our lenses try to capture its unfathomable atmosphere, as much as our adjectives make the same attempt. An army of others have tried before us. The arc leads from John Synge to the Beauty Queen of Leenaun. How photogenic those ruined cabins and deserted coastal villages. How marvellously lunar, all that Becketty barrenness.

Yet this coastline's elusiveness approaches the surreal. A currach rots on a shale-strewn strand, its crossbeams bleaching like the ribcage of a whale. A tumbledown pigsty is choked by wild rhododendrons. A rusting Edwardian bathtub on a bogside boreen is pressed into duty as water trough. From Douglas Hyde to Patrick Pearse, from Heinrich Boll to Richard Murphy, artists have encountered on the bleak western shores the banshee-muse that translates silence into beautiful image. But the making of images is an ambiguous enterprise. There are reasons why such a silence exists.

You would not think, as you amble the impossibly lovely waterfront at Cashel, that you might be walking over a burial ground. As you are stilled by the twilight descending on Dog's Bay, as you stroll the tidy fishing village laid out by Nimmo at Roundstone, it does not feel that you are moving through a space that was once a disaster zone: the Ground Zero, perhaps, of Victorian Europe. These beaches, those pebbled strands, saw astonishing suffering, as famine devastated the region in the 1840s. There was heroism, too; there was extraordinary courage. But this sea-land so hallowed by poet and tourist board alike witnessed tragedy so immense that many of those who observed it would be traumatised for ever by the sight.

The story told by Connemara's coastline is not part of modern Ireland's anthology of itself. Somehow, until recently, it had become an embarrassing bore. We thought it important not to dwell on that horrendous decade in which a million of the underclass died of famine. How old-fashioned, how uncosmopolitan to mention all that. Impolite, perhaps; a tad inconvenient. If we didn't forget the victims, we stewed their bones into propaganda, the meat of the murderous ballad and the lachrymose come-all-ye. But behind all the evasions were real men and women, children starved and dumped into pits. Their graves can still be discerned around the shorelands of Connemara: unmarked mounds, like middens for rubbish.

Abandoned by too many of the dominant of Ireland and Britain, masses of the desperate became refugees. We might call them 'asylum seekers' or 'economic migrants'. They were called scrounging layabouts by the commentariat of their day, a good number of whom regarded the landless Irish as subhuman. Government aid was insufficient: often too little, often too late. Many in Connemara fled their rotting homeland, drifting towards Galway to wait for the ships. The sea, which had supported some of them, became means of escape.

Like the age we inhabit now, this was an era of techno-logical advances, of artistic brilliance and scientific progress. Great novels were written; revolutions shook Europe; democracy budded; new engines were invented. But little of that trickled down to the starving of Connemara's coastline, as little enough of it matters now to the starving of Africa. The world was organised as a pyramid of power, with the affluent at the summit and the destitute bearing their weight. Then, as now, free-market politicians treated the poor to oratorical whip-cracks: inequality was regarded as economically progressive. Those who worked the hardest possessed the least wealth. Those who did nothing at all owned the most. With the wretched at the bottom were the nobodies of this shore-line: white Ethiopians of the Dickensian world.

Tens of thousands died. Entire families, sometimes. Within a few years the amazingly populous seaboard on which they lived would be decimated. A great many more would also have perished, but for the efforts of two gentle English people. James and Mary Ellis were a prosperous Quaker couple from the industrial city of Bradford. Despite having no apparent connection with Connemara, they moved from Yorkshire to what is now Letterfrack in 1849. There they paid for the building of homes and roads, a school, a store, a doctor's dispensary. They employed the locals fairly and treated them with dignity. 'A finer race of people no one could wish to see,' wrote Mary Ellis. 'Gentle, polite and easily made happy.'

The story of this coastline is incomplete without the Ellises, whose compassion altered its moral history as well as its geography. They believed that the world need not be a slum; that we live in a society, not just an economy; that every human life is unutterably precious. The imagery of holocaust is sometimes used about the Irish famine. If that's what it was, James and Mary Ellis are our Schindlers. The coastline they loved commands authentic memory. It is there to be read, and it has much to say.

On Cashel Hill, Connemara, there is a famine-era cemetery that is still in use today. Ard Caiseal looks down on a rock-strewn inlet that opens, dramatically, into the Atlantic. It is one of those loftily lonesome places that the folk music shared by Ireland and Appalachia somehow translates into sound. Oceanic windstorms buffet Cashel Hill; the trek up is dizzying and arduous. On the wintry afternoon I last made the climb, Christmas Eve 1999, a small stars-and-stripes pennant had been placed on a tombstone. It marked the grave of a young man of Connemara and Massachusetts, his surname a common one in this corner of Galway. He was twenty-one when he lost his life, very far from home. He should be alive today, dandling grand-children, but that was not to be his emigrant's fate. Locals recall that on the icy morning when his family and com-rades came to bury him, the jeep that bore his casket could not manage the steepness of Cashel Hill. So he was carried up the mountain to his final resting place, up the rocks to

Ard Caiseal, as his ancestors had been. He lies among those others whose names are long forgotten, who were abandoned in the latitudes of hunger.

His grave, and the desolate coastline that enspaces it, is a powerful reminder of many things: among them, the awful cost demanded by patriotism, the wrongs we have done to one another for love of country, the dreadful waste that is racism, all those unaccepted friendships, but the hope that the world can yet be a fairer place. If the text of Connemara's coastline includes any moral, it is a potent forewarning about hatred and bigotry. The sea divides. It also connects. Much depends on how you regard it. All who have found peace on this silent shore have something to learn from the stony words that commemorate him. In some sense they remember not only his own short life, but all the nameless who lie around him – wherever in the coastland of Connemara they lie, and in other Connemaras, across other seas.

L/CPL Peter Mary Nee:
United States Marine Corps
Born August 15, 1947
Died March 31, 1969
Vietnam

BIOGRAPHIES

SARAH BROWN

Sarah Brown is married to Gordon Brown, Chancellor of the Exchequer, and is President of the charity PiggyBankKids, which she founded in 2002. PiggyBankKids supports charitable projects that create opportunities for children and young people, and has launched the Jennifer Brown Research Fund to seek solutions to pregnancy difficulties and save newborn lives. Sarah is also Patron of the innovative educational charity, SHINE, and Patron of the Maggie's Cancer Caring Centre charity. Most recently, she became a Patron of the charity Women's Aid which works to keep women and children safe. Sarah and Gordon live in Fife and London with their son John.

GIL MCNEIL

Gil McNeil is Publishing Director for PiggyBankKids and has worked in advertising, the film business and publishing. She has written three novels: *The Only Boy for Me*, which is currently being adapted for television, *Stand By Your Man* and *In the Wee Small Hours*, which Bloomsbury will publish in 2005. Gil lives in Canterbury with her son.

HUGO TAGHOLM

Hugo Tagholm is Programme Director for PiggyBankKids. Hugo has worked in public relations and event management with a wide range of organisations, including the National Gallery, the Art Fund and the BBC. He lives in Camden Town and spends most of his spare time wakeboarding or chasing waves along the north Devon coast.

CHRIS HOOPER

Chris Hooper joined Special Olympics GB at the beginning of 2004 having spent almost seven years at the helm of the Special Olympics programme in New Zealand. Chris considers himself a quarter Kiwi and with his wife Sue and two young daughters lives near Tonbridge in Kent. Chris moved to New Zealand in 1993 having spent ten years working in the field of sport and leisure management.

ANDREW MOTION

Andrew Motion is Poet Laureate and Professor of Creative Writing at Royal Holloway College, University of London.

ALEXANDER MCCALL SMITH

Alexander McCall Smith is Professor of Medical Law at the University of Edinburgh, but is currently on leave to concentrate on his writing. He is the author of over fifty books on a wide range of subjects, but is best known for *The No. 1 Ladies' Detective Agency* series, translated into thirty-two languages worldwide. The first book in his new series, *The Sunday Philosophy Club*, has recently been published in the UK and USA. In his spare time he plays the bassoon in the RTO (Really Terrible Orchestra).

TRACY EDWARDS

Tracy Edwards successfully completed the 1990 Whitbread Round the World Race with the first all-female crew. Their yacht *Maiden* won two of the legs and went on to come second in class overall, the best result for a British boat since 1977. Tracy was voted Yachtsman of the Year and awarded an MBE. In 1998, again with an all-female crew, Tracy set out to beat the non-stop circumnavigation-of-the-world record and win the Jules Verne trophy. She was well on the way when her 92-foot catamaran was dismasted by a freak wave 2,000 miles off the coast of Chile. Tracy now lives in Doha, Qatar with her daughter, Mackenna, and has secured state sponsorship for a four-year sailing programme there. The Oryx Cup and the Quest will be the first ocean races based in the Middle East.

JOANNE HARRIS

Joanne Harris was born in Barnsley in 1964, of a French mother and an English father. She studied modern and medieval languages at St Catharine's College, Cambridge, after which she taught for fifteen years until the publication of her third novel, *Chocolat*, which was made into an academy award nominated movie in 2001. Since then she has written seven novels, a book of short stories, *Jigs & Reels*, and a cookbook, *The French Kitchen*, co-written with Fran Warde.

FI GLOVER

Fi Glover currently presents *Broadcasting House* on BBC Radio 4 on Sunday mornings. She has existed in a radio world for the last ten years, presenting the award-winning *Sunday Service* on Five Live as well as *The Fi Glover Show*. She has also presented the *Travel Show* on BBC 2, which inspired her to write her first book, *Travels With My Radio*. She also writes for the *Guardian*, *Independent* and various magazines.

ADMIRAL SIR ALAN WEST GCB DCS ADC

Born in 1948, Admiral Sir Alan West joined the Navy in 1965. He has spent the majority of his career at sea serving in fourteen different ships and commanding three of them. He was appointed as First Sea Lord and Chief of the Naval Staff in September 2002; this carries membership of the Defence Council and Admiralty Board. He is also the First and Principal Naval Aide-de-Camp to Her Majesty The Queen. He was made a GCB in the New Year's Honours List in 2004.

RUTH RENDELL

Ruth Rendell is the author of more than fifty novels, both in her own name and as Barbara Vine. Films have been made of two of her books, and Pedro Almodovar adapted her *Live Flesh* for the cinema. She was awarded the CBE in 1996 and a year later was made a life peer. Ruth Rendell lives in London and Suffolk, and has one son and two grandsons.

ALEX DICK READ

Alex Dick Read was born and raised in Tortola, British Virgin Islands, where he learned to love the ocean immediately. His surfing addiction began at 14-years-old and hasn't abated. After journalism training in London in the early 1990s, he returned to the Caribbean and worked for regional media, AP and Reuters. In 1997 he went to England to found and edit *The Surfer's Path*, a bi-monthly surf travel magazine. It now sells worldwide, placing a strong emphasis on world cultures and environmental issues. In 2003 it became the first 'green' surf mag, using 100 per cent post-consumer recycled paper and soya-based inks.

MARY LOUDON

Mary Loudon is the author of *Secrets & Lives, Middle England Revealed*; *Revelations, The Clergy Questioned*, and *Unveiled, Nuns Talking*. She has won four writing prizes, appeared frequently on radio and TV and contributed to three anthologies. She reviewed for *The Times* for five years. Mary is married, with two young daughters, and lives in Oxfordshire and the Wye valley. Her latest book, *Relative Stranger*, is published in 2005.

GERVASE PHINN

Professor Gervase Phinn is an author and poet. He is also a freelance lecturer, educational consultant, visiting professor of education and school inspector, and was voted Speaker of the Year in 2004. His books include *The Other Side of the Dale, Over Hill and Dale, Head Over Heels in the Dale,* and *Up and Down in the Dales* (which won the Customer Choice Award at the Spoken Books Awards), plus several children's anthologies and poetry books. Gervase is a Fellow of the Royal Society of Arts and Honorary Fellow of St John's College, York. He is married and a father of four.

JAMES LANDALE

James Landale is an experienced journalist who currently works as chief political correspondent for BBC News 24. Before joining the corporation in December 2002, he spent ten years at *The Times*. James has also messed around in boats most of his life. In 2000–01, he sailed from the UK to Hawaii in a round-the-world yacht race sponsored by *The Times*, his weekly dispatches describing the realities of life at sea. He lives with his wife, Cath, and daughter, Ellen, in south-west London.

SIR ROBIN KNOX-JOHNSTON

Sir Robin Knox-Johnston joined the Merchant Navy in 1957. In 1969, after 312 days at sea, he became the first person to sail around the world single-handedly and non-stop, in his 32-foot ketch *Suhaili*. In 1994 he won the Jules Verne Trophy for the fastest circumnavigation under sail: 75 days. He was president of the Sail Training Association, a youth development organisation, for nine years. He lives in Devon and still sails competitively.

JULIE MYERSON

Julie Myerson was born in Nottingham in 1960, read English at Bristol University and worked for the National Theatre and Walker Books before becoming a full-time writer. She has published five novels: *Sleepwalking*, *The Touch*, *Me & the Fat Man*, *Laura Blundy* and *Something Might Happen* (which was longlisted for the Man Booker Prize 2003). Her latest book is *HOME: The Story of Everyone Who Ever Lived in Our House* (HarperCollins). She and her partner Jonathan have three children, all of whom have grown up in the house in Clapham

DREW KAMPION

Drew Kampion is a former editor of *Surfer*, *Surfing*, *Wind Surf* and *Wind Tracks* magazines. He is the author of *The Book of Waves*, *Stoked: A History of Surf Culture*, *The Way of the Surfer*, *The Lost Coast* and *Waves: Echoes of the Storm*. A regular contributor to *The Surfer's Journal* and other magazines, he is currently American editor of *The Surfer's Path*, the first 'green' surf magazine. Married with two children, he lives on an island in Washington State.

MIKE GAYLE

Previously an agony uncle, Mike Gayle is a freelance journalist who has contributed to a variety of magazines including *FHM*, *Sunday Times Style* and *Cosmopolitan*. His five novels: *My Legendary Girlfriend*, *Mr Commitment*, *Turning Thirty*, *Dinner For Two* and *His 'n' Hers* have all been in the *Sunday Times* Top Ten bestsellers list. His new novel, *Brand New Friend*, is published in 2005.

LIBBY PURVES

Libby Purves is the author of ten novels, the latest being *Acting Up*, and various non-fiction works, including an account of sailing round Britain with children aged five and three, *One Summer's Grace*. She is also known as a *Times* columnist and presenter of Radio 4's *Midweek*. She was educated in Thailand, France, South Africa and Tunbridge Wells, and finally at St Anne's College, Oxford. Her children are now students.

SARAH WHITELEY

Sarah Whiteley is a former British, English and Junior European Champion surfer. She has spent the last ten years travelling and competing all over the world, searching for perfect waves along the way. Sarah has recently set up Walking on Waves surf school at Saunton Sands in north Devon with her partner Dave Meredith (*www.walkingonwaves.co.uk*).

RUSSELL CELYN JONES

Russell Celyn Jones is the author of five novels, including *Soldiers and Innocents* (David Higham Prize), *The Eros Hunter* (Society of Authors Award) and *Surface Tension*. His new novel, *Ten Seconds from the Sun*, is published in 2005. He is a staff reviewer for *The Times* and the Course Director of the MA in Creative Writing at Birkbeck College, London University. He was a Booker Prize judge in 2002.

PETER HILL

Peter Hill is a Glasgow-born artist and writer. In 2002 he exhibited his fictional artworks in the Sydney Biennale. In 2003 his book *Stargazing: Memoirs of a Young Lighthouse Keeper* was launched at the Edinburgh International Festival. His contribution to this anthology is drawn from his latest book, *Ocean Necklace: Journeys to the Lighthouses of Australia and New Zealand*. Peter Hill is the art critic for *The Sydney Morning Herald* and senior lecturer in the School of Creative Arts University of Melbourne.

ERICA WAGNER

Erica Wagner was born in New York and lives in London; she is the literary editor of *The Times*. Her stories have been widely anthologised and broadcast on the radio. Her books are *Gravity: Stories*, and *Ariel's Gift: Ted Hughes, Sylvia Plath and the Story of Birthday Letters*.

ALLAN WEISBECKER

Allan Weisbecker is a life-long surfer, novelist, screenwriter and award-winning photojournalist. His memoir, *In Search of Captain Zero*, reflects his profound love for the sea, which was passed to him by his father, an all-around waterman and poet. His short story in this anthology was inspired by his respect for commercial fishermen. Allan lives at the end of the road in outback Costa Rica, overlooking his own private perfect wave. For more of Allan's sea-related writings (and photographs) go to his website, *www.aweisbecker.com*. His newsletter about life in paradise is free.

JOSEPH O'CONNOR

Joseph O'Connor was born in Dublin. His books include the novels *Cowboys and Indians* (Whitbread Prize shortlist), *Desperadoes*, *The Salesman* and *Inishowen*. His most recent novel *Star of the Sea* received international acclaim and has sold upward of six hundred thousand copies to date. A number one bestseller in Britain and Ireland, it won the Prix Littéraire Européen Madeleine Zepter for European Novel of the Year, the Hennessy/Sunday Tribune Honorary 'Hall of Fame' Award, Italy's Premio Giuseppe Acerbi for Literary Fiction, France's Prix Millepages for Foreign Fiction, the Irish Post Award for Literature, a citation on the New York Public Library's prestigious annual '25 Books to Remember', an American Library Association 'Notable Book' listing, and was first runner-up in the British Book Awards 'Best Read' Category (voted by viewers of Channel 4's *Richard and Judy Book Club* programme). *Star of the Sea* is to be made into a film.

PiggyBankKids

PiggyBankKids is a charity that creates opportunities for children and young people who would otherwise miss out.

It is an umbrella charity that runs a number of projects, often in partnership with other charities. All its work is in the UK.

PiggyBankKids's work includes:

The Jennifer Brown Research Fund

The Jennifer Brown Research Fund has created a new research laboratory in Edinburgh to solve pregnancy difficulties and save newborn lives. The fund finances four separate research projects – looking at pre-eclampsia, early labour problems, curing blindness in premarutre babies and reducing incidences of brain damage in premature babies.

PiggyBankKids has recently launched a new popular appeal to raise a further £1 million to continue support for this research. Designed around the theme of babies smiling, the appeal will combine 'Smile' with 'Million' to become the 'Search for a Smillion' campaign, and will be featured on our website and in our newsletters during 2005.

The Big Night In

Launched in 2004 this fundraising initiative invites people to host a party or an event at home. Our next Big Night In is scheduled for Thursday 10 November 2005. All money raised during the Big Night In goes directly to projects ranging from the Jennifer Brown Research Fund to mentoring and family support services and charities focusing on improving sports provision for vulnerable young people.

Mentoring and volunteering

PiggyBankKids works with a number of charity partners supporting the mentoring of young people providing fundraising, PR and marketing advice. To support this work we published *Moving On Up*, edited by Sarah Brown, where famous people wrote about the mentors who had most influenced their lives. Free copies of *Moving On Up* were sent to every state and independent secondary school in the UK.

Child Poverty

PiggyBankKids has given grants to a number of charities including one-parent families and family service units, and edited two anthologies of stories, *Magic* and *Summer Magic*, both published by Bloomsbury, with royalties going to one-parent families.

Sports Provision

PiggyBankKids is supporting Special Olympics Great Britain – which provides sports facilities for young people with learning difficulties – with the publication of this book.

You can read more about PiggyBankKids projects at *www.piggybankkids.org*

Special Olympics
Great Britain

MISSION OF SPECIAL OLYMPICS

The mission of Special Olympics is to provide a year-round programme of sports training and competition for people with a learning disability, giving each person, regardless of their ability, the opportunity to develop physical fitness, demonstrate courage, experience joy and participate in a sharing of skills and friendship with their families, other Special Olympics athletes and the community.

BACKGROUND

Special Olympics was founded in the USA in 1968 and now has programmes in more than 150 countries throughout the world.

Special Olympics Great Britain was established in 1978 and annually caters for over 7,000 athletes. It has 600 registered coaches and 2,000 volunteers actively and regularly taking part in England, Scotland and Wales.

Special Olympics GB is a Registered Charity (no. 800329).

SPORTS TRAINING AND COMPETITION

Special Olympics seeks to provide the highest possible quality of coaching and competition for its athletes. Athletes are able to choose which sports they would like to participate in from a range of more than twenty-six summer and winter sports.

Special Olympics world games are organised every two years, alternating between summer and winter games. At the 1999 World Summer Games, GB was the largest team from outside the USA, with 147 athletes competing in fourteen sports. In 2003 the World Summer Games was held in Dublin and SOGB sent a team of 260.

Special Olympics GB organises national summer games every four years. In the intervening years local, regional and national single-sport competitions are staged. SOGB also has the opportunity to enter teams into European Special Olympics events.

STRUCTURE OF SPECIAL OLYMPICS GB

The majority of Special Olympics training and competition is organised by a network of more than 130 locally based groups. Groups also affiliate to one of ten regions in England (corresponding to the Sport

England Regions), eight regions in Scotland or to Special Olympics Wales.

WHAT MAKES SPECIAL OLYMPICS SPECIAL?

All Special Olympics competition is 'banded'. This allows all athletes the opportunity for achievement based on their own level of ability. This philosophy is carried right through to the selection of teams for international events, where all athletes and not just the elite have the chance to be chosen to represent GB.

Special Olympics therefore gives opportunities for athletes with a learning disability of all ability levels. Apart from the normal Special Olympics programme in team and individual sports, Special Olympics also offers Unified Sports to promote the inclusion of athletes with a learning disability into mainstream sport, and the Motor Activities Training Programme for people with profound or multiple disabilities.

EMPOWERMENT

Special Olympics is committed to the process of empowering people with a learning disability and is seeking to involve its athletes in decision-making processes at all levels of the organisation. Special Olympics also provides opportunities for its athletes to qualify as sports leaders, coaches and officials.

PARTNERSHIPS

Special Olympics GB is committed to working in partnership with other agencies to further promote opportunities for people with a learning disability.

OUR GOAL IS CLEAR

To involve 5,000 new athletes, 1,000 new volunteers and 400 new coaches by the end of 2006, and to raise £1 million to fund this aggressive growth. This will enable us to appoint a much-needed regional development structure at grassroots level, including appointment of regional development officers to support our indefatigable volunteers and increase awareness of our programme and the abilities of those with learning disabilities. We want to increase outreach to schools and universities, both mainstream and learning disability, and promote attitudes of acceptance and inclusion of people with learning disabilities in the community.

For further information please visit *www.specialolympicsgb.org* or contact the National Development Office at 18 Grosvenor Gardens, London SW1W ODH. Telephone: 020 7824 7800. Fax: 020 7824 7801. Email: karensogb@aol.com